To

From

Date

Walking
- in -
Wonder

A DEVOTIONAL JOURNAL
FOR MOMS OF TODDLERS

CATHERINE CLAIRE LARSON

THOMAS NELSON

Since 1798

Walking in Wonder

© 2024 Catherine Claire Larson

Published in Nashville, Tennessee, by Thomas Nelson. Thomas Nelson is a registered trademark of HarperCollins Christian Publishing, Inc.

Published in association with The Bindery Agency, www.TheBinderyAgency.com.

Thomas Nelson titles may be purchased in bulk for educational, business, fund-raising, or sales promotional use. For information, please email SpecialMarkets@ThomasNelson.com.

Any internet addresses, phone numbers, or company or product information printed in this book are offered as a resource and are not intended in any way to be or to imply an endorsement by Thomas Nelson, nor does Thomas Nelson vouch for the existence, content, or services of these sites, phone numbers, companies, or products beyond the life of this book.

ISBN 978-1-4002-3620-6 (audiobook)
ISBN 978-1-4002-3619-0 (eBook)
ISBN 978-1-4002-3615-2 (HC)

Printed in Malaysia
24 25 26 27 28 COS 10 9 8 7 6 5 4 3 2 1

Contents

Introduction

A few days after David, my fifth son, blew out the candle on his first birthday cake and smeared frosting across his deliciously chubby cheeks, my husband and I left our other four children in the capable hands of their grandparents and skedaddled for a few days' getaway to celebrate our tenth wedding anniversary. We decided to take our one-year-old with us because he wasn't weaned yet, and truly he wouldn't be much trouble. He wasn't. My husband snapped a picture of him snuggled close to my chest in his baby carrier as we took a walk across a mile-high suspension bridge at Grandfather Mountain in North Carolina. I remember the next day Baby Boy taking in the dazzling colors of the Chihuly glass sculptures floating in the ponds of the luscious gardens at the Biltmore House from the comfort of his stroller. And later, while it was still summer twilight, David went to bed in his playpen, all worn out and wearing his light-weight footed pajamas. It gave my husband and me ample time to sit and enjoy a sunset on the deck of our cabin and the fireflies that followed. Looking back on those days, I recall that our little boy was still very much a baby, from pacifier to naps to cuddles.

The year that followed passed by in a blur in many ways: homeschooling three older children and keeping a preschooler busy. In the midst of it, we made a cross-country move; traveled with my oldest, Luke, on his first experience at a global STEM competition; celebrated my second-born son Isaiah's silver baseball trophy; watched my middle guy, James, learn to read; and cheered Beau, the three-year-old, as he dashed to first base at his first T-ball game.

The changes that year were tremendous, but they paled in comparison to the changes in our youngest. We'd gotten too used to this ordinary miracle to think it so extraordinary. But in the space of a year, my baby began to blossom into a boy. My oldest son coaxed him into walking using two crayons, Luke holding the top of the crayon and baby David holding the bottom. Baby David went from pursing his lips at sweet potatoes to downing taco meat and cheese at an alarming rate. By year's end, with Isaiah's steady hand, David was balancing on a scooter, hitting a Wiffle ball James gently tossed at him, and climbing the tree house ladder behind Beau.

I have a photo taken a day after David's second birthday. I'm beaming as my sweaty little one cuddles up in my lap. The moment lasted only a few seconds—one of those apparitions of the camera making the fleeting moment seem endless. He was sweaty because he had been go-go-going up until that moment. I was smiling because I had gotten a sweet moment of snuggles with him before he rebounded with renewed energy for more boyish adventures with his big brothers. As I think about those moments a year apart—the baby snuggled in the baby carrier with Mom and Dad as we crossed a mile-high suspension bridge and the sweaty boy taking a momentary reprieve in my lap before running off—the changes are staggering. In a year, he changed from baby to little boy. I don't say this with regret but rather awe.

What a privilege it is to see this transformation from total dependence to burgeoning independence. Sure, they say, "Blink, and you'll miss it." But that's true of any wonder: a sunset, a storm coming in over the ocean, a falling star. The very fact that you are watching a metamorphosis—a change in motion, in time—is part of what makes it so mesmerizing. The very transience of the thing itself is part of its beauty. You know it won't last, but ah . . . isn't that part of what makes it so breathtaking?

Older mothers will tell you to "savor it." And in the midst of toddler tantrums, sleep deprivation, cleaning strewn food from the floor, or picking out the dried oatmeal flakes stuck in baby's hair, we all may very well roll our eyes at the "savor it" remark as the sentimentalizing schmaltz of someone who is distant from the mess and monotony of toddlers. Yet deep down, as much as it may irk us sometimes to hear those two words, we know there is something too true about those sentiments.

But how do we savor it? How do we appreciate a slow-motion miracle? I think we ourselves must slow down. It isn't a perpetual slowing. (There are some moments we don't really want to savor after all: the tantrum, the diaper rash, the 3 a.m. night terror, the defiant no.) But it is a habit of slowing for moments at a time to stop and simply be present, to tune in and enjoy the enjoyable in the present moment—the miracle of metamorphosis in progress.

We must look, listen, smell, and touch what is right before us. You did it when you were falling in love: you looked at your beloved over a candlelit table, you enjoyed the sound of his voice or his laughter, you caught yourself breathing him in as you hugged him tightly and found even the feel of his hand in yours strangely comforting.

Now, as we fall in love with our little ones, there will be no candlelight and likely very little quiet. And it will by no means be all rose petals and moonlight. But we can still take regular moments to stop and pay attention: to enjoy the sight of the perfect little curl on her forehead, to listen to the delighted squeal of excitement in her block tower, to smell that baby-shampooed head nestled under your chin for a story, or to delight in the chubby little hand that grabs your own for comfort. They won't all be perfect moments, but we can find beauty in the moments we have and treasure them.

One of the reasons I have written this devotional journal is that I think this discipline of slowing down and paying attention is not only what we must do to savor our children but also what we must do to savor God. We must regularly take moments of deliberate slowness to appreciate and delight in the beloved. And here's the beauty of it: The process of pausing and praising changes you. It reorients you from worn to grateful. It takes your gaze off of yourself. It reenergizes you for the work ahead.

While God has certainly made our children worthy of wonder, He alone commands our utter awe. He is unchanging. And yet in His infinite complexity, we could spend all eternity gazing on Him and never plumb the depths of the delight of knowing Him.

Here is another wonder: He, too, is involved in a slow-motion miracle of metamorphosis. It is the change that is happening in you and in me as His children. This is a miracle of grace and sanctification. Blink and you may miss it. You are changing from infant into mature believer. And guess what? You better believe that God is delighting in watching you grow. Do you love those moments when your little one has fallen asleep in your arms? When you find yourself still rocking her and singing a favorite lullaby over her, just enjoying her—savoring her? The Bible says in Zephaniah 3:17 (NIV) that the Lord "will take great delight in you," and in His love He "will rejoice over you with singing." You, too, are a miracle in motion, a glorious metamorphosis in progress.

So here in the pages of this devotional journal, I invite you to stop regularly and pay attention. I invite you to pay attention to your amazing and glorious God who has already done so much for you and is still not finished. I invite you to come into His presence and praise Him and pray to Him and be changed by that time with Him. I long to see you energized for your days by the enjoyment of being in His presence. I yearn to see you stop and savor Him in all His beauty and goodness, and so be transformed by that contemplation.

I also invite you to use these pages to slow down and savor the wonder of the unfolding marvel that is your little one. May this book be a constant reminder to be present, to pay attention when in your child's presence. And as you take the time to write prayers and ordinary memories, you will be savoring the moments that make this year so special. You will be creating a remembrance of the ordinary, extraordinary work that you had the privilege to witness.

I think you will also be paying attention to another wonder. When Jesus called the little children to Himself, He said, "Let the little children come to me, and do not hinder them, for the kingdom of heaven belongs to such as these" (Matthew 19:14 NIV). In some mysterious, bigger-than-my-understanding way, God wants to teach us something of His kingdom by observing the way of a child.

So I hope you will take this invitation. This book invites you to regularly take time out to invest in your own spiritual growth so that you might not just survive these exhausting days of young motherhood but truly thrive. This book is not meant to be one more burden to your already too-tired self, but rather a tiny oasis in the midst of motherhood. I've pulled twelve themes from the Bible to focus on each month; each theme works on two levels: babyhood and our own spiritual walk. These themes remind us how, like a child, we, too, grow in grace, feeding on Christ, imitating Him, learning to walk in Him, and much more. Hopefully, as you nourish your own spiritual growth and delight in the love of your heavenly Father, you will be renewed to take a piece of that calm back into your hectic world. This journal will serve as a place to mark both your own growth in grace and your child's physical growth, and to marvel at both your milestones and theirs. It will be a place where you are reminded that you take part in the holiest and most noble kind of work. By the time you are done, whether all the pages are neatly filled or many days remain untouched by your pen, you will have a keepsake of love to pass on to your child one day. It will show your child that their mother loved them so much, she took time out to grow in her faith because that was the very best thing she could do for them. Their mother, though not perfectly, sought to stop and savor her God and stop and savor the miracle of them. What a beautiful gift to give!

Note to Reader: It's so hard to write a journal like this knowing that the moms who are reading it will be facing so many varied circumstances. I apologize in advance that I can't speak directly to every situation—to the single mom struggling to parent alone, to the mom of a special-needs child whose toddler will not reach many of these developmental milestones, to the foster parent or adoptive parent whose story is just a bit different. Whatever your situation, please know that though I can't speak to your heart directly, I trust that God will take my feeble efforts here and speak the specific words you need to hear. Also, for all my readers, I've done my best to present information about developmental milestones and tips for you as a parent, but I'm not a doctor, and any advice or information in this book does not constitute any health or medical advice. Consult your own child's pediatrician with any questions you may have. Thanks for reading, and I pray that this book is a blessing to your life and your child's.

ONE
Walking

Your Twelve-Month-Old,

Developmental Guide

I t's hard to believe that your little one may very well have tripled in size since just one year ago and may already be a good two and a half feet tall when pulling up to full height on the furniture. Don't worry if that growth pace slows down a little around this time; that is normal. Whether your little one is scooting, army crawling, pulling up, cruising (the term for moving while holding on to something), or walking, there are sure to be more strides toward independence this month. (And if your little one is not walking, relax. Lots of twelve-month-olds are more comfortable crawling until thirteen or fourteen months, or later.)

You may also notice your little one's hand-eye coordination improving. That's because his or her eyesight is now on adult levels and keener than ever. That means more finger foods are actually getting into the mouth these days and less on the floor. That's good news.

Speaking of food, your child may be starting to enjoy a variety of foods these days, especially with all those new pearly whites popping through. Try giving him or her a sampling of the foods you like to eat, only in smaller-sized pieces. Fruits, cooked veggies, bits of ground beef or soft fish—this is a great time to expand her palate. But be prepared for your toddler to show some definite preferences for what he likes and doesn't. He will likely consume about one thousand calories per day at this point, about half of which will still come from breast milk or formula, and eventually perhaps cow's milk, which will help provide vitamin D.

With all those foods and milk, make sure you are completing a regimen of brushing those little teeth that are appearing. You especially don't want to fall into the bad habit of letting a little one fall asleep with a bottle or sippy cup of milk or drink other than water.

That nighttime routine is important. Reading picture books with your toddler will help her grow in vocabulary and connection with you. Encourage her to fall asleep on her own and let her learn ways to self-soothe. By now she should be sleeping about twelve to sixteen hours a day, divided up between nighttime sleep and usually two naps that may vary in length from thirty minutes to two hours. Like your little one, those naps will begin changing soon. Enjoy those precious minutes of downtime! It's a great time to catch up on your to-dos, but also to connect with your good God.

Developmental Highlight: Walking

WHAT TO EXPECT

Healthy children will develop at different rates, and while many children will take their first steps around their first birthday, not to worry; many more will wait a couple of months before reaching this milestone. Personality and genetics play a role. Some kids are naturally more cautious, others more risk tolerant. One thing to ease your mind either way: studies show that there is no correlation between early walking and better coordination or cognition later in life. So if your child is a late bloomer, don't panic, but do discuss it with your doctor if your baby hasn't walked by eighteen months.

HOW TO HELP

How can you encourage your baby if he or she is not walking? First, if your child is already an adept crawler, there may be little motivation to try walking. You can help by moving some interesting toys up off the floor and on to a sofa or coffee table. Or sit a little distance away from your child and put a chair or something sturdy near him to pull up on. Once he's pulled up, show him something interesting where you are, hold out your hands, and encourage him to try walking toward you.

Also, make sure your little one is getting ample time on the floor. Spending too much time sitting in high chairs or strollers, or even spending all their time in your arms may discourage them from building the muscle, balance, and coordination to take those first steps. A sturdy push toy with a wide, heavy base and slow-moving wheels can be a good motivation and help as well.

THE MECHANICS

Little ones learning to walk are called toddlers because of their characteristic gait. You will notice that early walkers tend to hold their arms straight out and keep their legs wide apart, pausing between steps to think about the motion. They may jerk from side to side, moving one foot at a time. By about six months after they begin walking, this hesitating gait begins to mature into a more controlled movement. Their hands will be at their side, their feet closer together, and they will step in a way that looks more natural—heel to toe. If you don't see this kind of maturation, or if your child always walks only on toes by about eighteen months, talk to your doctor. But wherever your toddler is in the journey toward mobility, enjoy the moment and celebrate each move in the right direction.

This Month's Spiritual Focus: Walking with God

Just as your babe is learning to walk, this is a great month to focus on what Scripture teaches us as believers about what it means to walk in God's ways. Like your little one, you will often stumble. Be patient with yourself, remembering that growing in grace is a process.

Walk and Not Grow Weary

*Even youths grow tired and weary, and
young men stumble and fall; but those who
hope in the LORD will renew their strength.*
ISAIAH 40:30–31 NIV

It seems like just yesterday you were snuggling that downy-headed newborn in your arms, and now the candle on that first birthday cake has been blown out! But if that first year whizzed by, then buckle your seat belt for the wild ride that is toddlerhood. Did you know that the average toddler expends the same amount of energy per day per ounce of body weight as an adult who runs thirty miles? No wonder you feel exhausted keeping up with him!

But if you are feeling run down, remember you aren't alone. In today's passage we are reminded that "even youths grow tired and weary." All of us mamas will face exhaustion. But just a few verses before today's passage, Isaiah reminds us that God doesn't "grow tired or weary, and his understanding"—His deep compassion and knowing of us—"no one can fathom" (Isaiah 40:28 NIV). God's strength is perfect despite our imperfect strength. And while others may not understand what you are facing today, He not only understands but offers you compassion.

Wherever you are on your spiritual journey, as we "hope in the Lord"—that is, as we exercise our confident faith in the truth of His Word and promises—God renews our strength. He gives us made-new strength for the cares of this day. Hope in the Lord. And, by His grace, keep going in the right direction: toward Him.

Walk with the Wise

*Blessed is the one who does not walk
in step with the wicked . . . but whose
delight is in the law of the LORD, and who
meditates on his law day and night.*
PSALM 1:1–2 NIV

You may be one year into this parenting journey or much further along, but have you ever stopped to think about your goal as a parent? The first psalm paints this glorious image of a tree planted beside the waters, whose roots are continually soaking up the water from that constant nearby source of nourishment and whose limbs stretch out, giving shade to the weary. This tree is the emblem of a close and nourished Christian life—flourishing. It is an image for you, dear mother, to hold close and seek not only for yourself, but also for your little sapling. With God's help, one day your son or daughter may grow to be that life-giving, shade-creating, fruit-bearing tree!

But before we can influence their walk, we must start with our own. And here the first word of caution from the psalmist is to "not walk in step with the wicked." Who or what is influencing you? To what voices are you listening? Maybe you don't hang out with a corrupting crowd, but perhaps you invite godless, foul-mouthed, sexually immoral people into your mind by saturating it with certain kinds of television or movies. We can't change the people in these media streams, but they can and do change us.

Instead, the Scriptures invite us to walk in the company of the wise and grow wise. Fill your mind with His Word; meditate on it day and night. Plant your life near the wellspring of life, and you won't have to merely survive these toddler years—your soul can flourish.

Walk in *All* His Ways

*And now, Israel, what does the LORD your
God require of you, but to fear the LORD
your God, to walk in all His ways and to
love Him, to serve the LORD your God with
all your heart and with all your soul.*
DEUTERONOMY 10:12

Have you ever been asked to do something that you knew from the outset you just couldn't accomplish? If you're like me, with a toddler in the house, you may feel like you can't accomplish a complete sentence, let alone that daunting project. Such is life with a toddler! When I was in school, every year there was the Presidential Fitness Test. Every year, I'd get through the sit-ups, mile run, and shuttle run. I'd crush the flexibility requirement, but then it would come to the chin-ups. Every year, I knew before we even began that I was doomed.

When I look at this command from God to His people, to walk in all His ways, to love Him with all my heart and all my soul and keep the whole of the commandments, I'm prone to feel the same way I did about that chin-up bar: doomed to fail. But here's the beauty of it: Our failure—our inability to keep the whole of the law—is exactly where God wants us to start. He wants us to realize our utter need of Him. And then He wants to meet us in that need with Jesus, our elite spiritual athlete, the perfect One who has perfectly kept this requirement for us. Without Him, we're lost when it comes to keeping this or any of His commandments. But through Him, we're empowered to do what otherwise we would be too weak to accomplish.

The first step in learning to walk in all His ways is acknowledging that we need His grace, His power, and His will for each and every step.

Your little one recently had a birthday! Stop and take a few minutes to record some favorite moments from that day. What in particular do you want to remember and savor?

_____

_____

_____

_____

_____

_____

Oh goodness, it is hard to see our toddlers flail and be frustrated, whether it's learning to walk or trying to communicate. Write a prayer for yourself as you deal with your little one in these moments of frustration and meltdown. Ask God to help you be compassionate and patient.

_____

_____

_____

_____

_____

_____

Our God Who Taught Us to Walk

"I myself taught Israel how to walk, leading him along by the hand. But he doesn't know or even care that it was I who took care of him."
HOSEA 11:3 NLT

My first son took his good, sweet time before he decided to start walking. The day he really wanted the graham crackers on the other side of the room, well, that was the day he finally walked. Eight years later, I watched him teach his youngest brother (at the time) to walk, bent over him in love, his other brothers cheering every step. There is something so deeply exhilarating and bonding about being part of this milestone. We cheer, catch, coax, and cajole, and yet it is an unseen labor of love that our children will not remember one day.

Do you know God has been at work in your life in ways you can't even remember? As pastor John Piper wrote, "God is always doing ten thousand things in your life and you are only vaguely aware of three of them."[1] The point isn't the numbers (who can know?) but the sentiment. God is always up to much more than we can fathom. This should give us such great comfort. My favorite chapter of the Bible is Hosea 11. In it God details His passionate love for His people. How He loved them from the very beginning, even teaching them to walk, but how they turned from Him. The chapter culminates in how God refuses to give up on them, how He will roar like a lion and how His people will come trembling.

Your God is always working in your life, and in your child's life, whether you see it, remember it, or even feel it. His work is constant. His passion is a given. What comfort this gives us today!

Walk by the Spirit

*But I say, walk by the Spirit, and you will
not gratify the desires of the flesh. . . . For
these are opposed to each other, to keep you
from doing the things you want to do.*
GALATIANS 5:16–17 ESV

I remember the very first time I watched my child willfully disobey me. He had recently learned to walk, and we were out for a summer evening stroll in the neighborhood. He was putting his brand-new shoes to good use. We were rounding a corner, and the sidewalk split. If my toddler went straight, he would head toward a dangerous road. If he followed the turn, he'd head home. He was about two yards ahead of my pregnant-again self, and I called out for him to stop. Instead, he turned his head, looked at me with a look of understanding, then paused and kept doing what he wanted to do: head toward the busy street. I had plenty of time to stop him, but I still remember the sinking feeling.

Like my son, sometimes I take a look over my shoulder when God calls me to stop, and I keep right on going. All of us at times feel that war within ourselves between what feels good and what we know is right. But here's the truth: sin feels good temporarily, but in the end it enslaves us. As Paul said a few verses earlier, "You were called to freedom" (Galatians 5:13 ESV), and the truest freedom is not being chained to our selfish wants and lusts but set free to give and to serve others out of love. So when you are standing at the crossroads, perhaps you can hear in your ears not a killjoy's no but a parent's cry of care. He wants what is best for you, and what is best is diametrically opposed to the sin that ensnares us. "For freedom Christ has set us free" (v. 1 ESV).

11

Walk in Step

*If we live by the Spirit, let us also
keep in step with the Spirit.*
GALATIANS 5:25 ESV

A side from the sometimes-loud noise of sirens, my toddlers have always loved parades. In our midsize town, we have them regularly: the Fourth of July, Thanksgiving, Christmas, and Memorial Day. It seems like anytime is a good excuse for a parade. And while the strewn candy and fire trucks are always a hit, the marching bands are quite thrilling as well. There's a beauty that we don't see every day in keeping in perfect step with the one before you. Often we come home and keep up the game with the help of that classic children's song from Peter Pan, "Following the Leader."

Like the parade marchers, we are called to keep in step with the Spirit, not running ahead or lagging behind. We run ahead of God when we don't stop to pray and seek God's face with our decisions. Lagging behind is when we find ourselves reluctant to do His will, and we put it off or do it half-heartedly. We keep in step as we align our will and our ways to His. Walking in Christ means having a consciousness of Him in our daily lives. Imagine you were in a marching band—and to your left is Christ, to your right is Christ, in front of you is Christ, and behind you is Christ. Each way you turn, you see Him. How motivated you'd be to keep in step with Him! This is the kind of consciousness we are to have as we seek to walk this life—looking constantly at His example and then modeling our own steps after His. But the good news is we have help in doing this! Because not only is Christ all around us, but if we are His, then the Holy Spirit dwells within us. That means the Spirit will nudge us from the inside if we are out of step and will help us realign. As we cooperate with the Spirit and align our steps to the beat, we abound in the fruit of the Spirit mentioned in this chapter of Galatians (5:22–23). The more we keep in time, the more our children and others will want to catch that beautiful rhythm and follow along.

Where is your little one these days in his quest for mobility? Is he scooting, crawling, cruising along furniture, taking his first steps, or already well on his way to walking? Don't worry about where your little one is, but rather celebrate it. Record it here and savor this snapshot in time.

_____

_____

_____

_____

What practices in your life help you keep in step with the Spirit? Are there habits that could help you stay more continually in line with Him throughout the day?

_____

_____

_____

_____

When You Walk Along the Way

You shall teach them [God's commandments] diligently to your children, and shall talk of them when you sit in your house, when you walk by the way, when you lie down, and when you rise up.
DEUTERONOMY 6:7

I wish I could remind each mother I know, every single day, of the high and holy calling of motherhood. Our culture reduces motherhood to its lowest common denominator: physical duties that can be easily outsourced. Motherhood is so much more. Motherhood is nurturing living souls who are of inestimably great importance to our Father. In fact, God charges mothers and fathers alike with this command of grave importance: "Love the Lord your God with all your heart, with all your soul, with all your mind, and with all your strength" (Mark 12:30), and we are to teach this and His commandments to our children. He wants us to talk about those commands when we sit, when we walk, when we lie down, when we rise up. In other words, *all* the time!

Your toddler is still too young to understand much, but you can begin now to build the atmosphere in your home with rhythms and routines. For instance, in the morning or evening you can have a habit of singing a song about God and reading a Bible picture book together. You can play uplifting Christian music in your house to set the tone. You can be a part of a church community and make regular weekly worship, serving others, and community fellowship a habit now that will continue for years to come. And most importantly, *you* can grow in *your* wholehearted mind, body, and soul love of God so that it permeates you.

Walking in Integrity

The righteous lead blameless lives;
blessed are their children after them.
PROVERBS 20:7 NIV

Yesterday we read the famous command from God in Deuteronomy to teach our children diligently. Even before our toddlers are old enough to listen to long Bible stories or memorize scriptures, they are watching and imitating our walk. Today's verse reminds us that the righteous walk with integrity. Integrity is when our words and actions match, and it is the motivation in our hearts to do what is right, no matter the cost. What would you do if you knew you could get away with it? Hopefully, your answer to this is constrained not by those watching but by your love for Jesus Christ. This and not external motivation is what gives us such a firm resolve to do what is right, even when it is costly. Integrity *will* cost us: it will move us to ask for forgiveness when it would be easier not to. It will move us to change a private behavior to match our public confession or to speak our conscience when it would be easier to just stay quiet. You won't do this perfectly. But the person of integrity is consistently trying to align her faith and her actions because of her love for God.

Today's proverb tells us that the children of those with integrity are blessed after them. This doesn't mean that your children will inherit your faith; it does mean that your children will experience blessings in their lives because of the integrity of your life. There will be an overflow. I continually marvel at the head start I have in life simply because my parents loved Jesus and created a stable home for me. Your walk of faith will have a ripple effect, not just on your child, but on a thousand generations after you (Exodus 20:5–6). Amazing!

15

For the Joy Set Before You

*I have no greater joy than to hear
that my children walk in truth.*
3 JOHN 1:4

People always say, "Blink and you'll miss it." That's because kids grow so fast. You've seen it already: one-year-olds have usually tripled their birth weight and grown around twelve inches (or one to one and a half inches per month) since birth. Astonishing! The time will go fast; that's why, as we continue meditating on walking in God's ways, I want to share a verse of vision-casting with you. John wrote, "I have no greater joy than to hear that my children walk in truth." The height of his joy was to hear that his (spiritual) children were walking in God's truth. How much more so should this be our aim for our own children!

While none of us are guaranteed tomorrow, I hope you will see the next seventeen years or so, if the Lord allows, with your son or daughter under your roof as a time of intense discipleship. This is a time to invest daily in their hearts, minds, and spirits. When your toddler is little, you will pour in thousands of hours of simply serving his basic needs and filling his heart with love. Every day you do this, you model Christ, who washed His disciples' feet and considered no job too menial. But as your little one grows, you will fill him with God's Word, talking daily about life through a Christian worldview lens. Seize those roughly six thousand days. Jesus endured the cross "for the joy that was set before Him" (Hebrews 12:2). As you pour your life into the discipleship of your child, do it with great joy and with the hope of one day seeing your grown son or daughter walking in God's truth.

Now is a great time to cast a vision for your future. What practices, routines, and rhythms do you hope will be a part of your home as your child grows that will create an atmosphere where they will learn to walk in God's ways? Dream about the spiritual environment you want to cultivate in your home.

_____

_____

_____

_____

_____

_____

What steps do you need to begin taking now to build the kind of atmosphere in your home where your child will thrive spiritually? Are there spiritual habits you need to begin cultivating now in your own personal life? Is there knowledge you need to gain? How can you set a solid foundation?

_____

_____

_____

_____

_____

_____

_____

When You Pass Through the Waters

*"When you pass through the waters,
I will be with you; and through the
rivers, they shall not overflow you."*
ISAIAH 43:2

A s our children begin walking, we mamas have a way of staying close at hand to assist. We know there will be lots of falls. We know there are dangers all around. We have compassion *and* understanding. How much more so can we expect our God to hover over us! Whatever trials, persecutions, or sorrows you face, you do not walk through them alone if you are a follower of Jesus.

"When you pass through the waters, I will be with you," God promises. This is such a great verse for us mamas to remember. I know there are times when we feel overwhelmed, as if we've been inundated—flooded. God promises to be with us. Remember how He was with the Israelites in the days of Moses? The sea before them, raging chariots behind them—what would they do? "But the children of Israel had walked on dry land in the midst of the sea, and the waters were a wall to them on their right hand and on their left" (Exodus 14:29). God did not abandon them. He did not let the waters flood them. And neither will He abandon you or me. He walks with us in our troubles. He sent His Son, Jesus—our Emmanuel, God with us—as a constant reminder: we do not walk alone.

A Maturing Walk

*[We ask] that you may walk worthy
of the Lord, fully pleasing Him, being
fruitful in every good work and
increasing in the knowledge of God.*
COLOSSIANS 1:10

When our little ones learn to walk, they sure do make us giggle. There is a reason toddlers are called toddlers. Their uneven, uncertain steps with their arms held out in front for balance make for one adorable baby Frankenstein. Day by day, however, we watch in awe as their balance, coordination, and even risk-taking grows. What a delight it is to see those little uneven steps come toward us or propel them to new adventures that weren't possible days or weeks before.

Likewise, in our spiritual walk we should notice maturation. As Paul said here in this passage, we should see both our knowledge and our fruit increasing. Head, heart, and hands are interconnected. As our understanding of God's Word and His ways grows, our hearts *and* our actions should be changing. Paul prayed for this for the Colossians, knowing that this kind of fruit isn't the result of just *trying* harder. It is God's grace freely poured out as we find ourselves "strengthened with all might, according to His glorious power" (v. 11). Why? Did you catch that fleeting reference in verse 10? Paul prayed that we "may walk worthy . . . fully pleasing Him." Our growth in spiritual maturity pleases our God. Can you fathom that somehow in His providence, He has ordered things such that you and I can bring Him delight? As we mature from crawling to cruising, from walking to running, let us press on to delight our good God!

Walk in the Good Works Prepared for You

We are His workmanship, created in Christ Jesus for good works, which God prepared beforehand that we should walk in them.
EPHESIANS 2:10

Our library has lovely grab-and-go bags for moms of toddlers and preschoolers. Inside the brown paper bag are instructions for a craft and all the materials already cut out and ready. The craft may tie into a certain classic picture book or favorite kids movie, and it's all ready for me to pick up and go. I bring it home and feel like a supermom with a craft and book ready for them. The librarians have clearly put some forethought into stimulating a lovely educational experience.

This passage in Ephesians kind of reminds me of my library's grab-and-go crafts. Somewhere in eternity past, God foreknew that I would be His and that He would use me for His purposes. As I walk through my life, there are moments when the good works are already laid out for me. All I have to do is grab and go, so to speak, knowing that He's prepared everything in advance, including me. That's comforting to realize. It also makes these opportunities that much harder to ignore. God's done all the prep work; all He asks of me is that I show up and walk in the ways He's already set out for me.

Have you sensed God nudging you to some good work? If so, don't be anxious; trust that He has equipped and prepared you and will strengthen you "with all might" (Colossians 1:11) to do all He plans through you.

When you think back on this past year with your little one, what one memory brings the biggest smile to your face? Write down that moment and thank God for the privilege of being the one to walk in wonder with your little one through these days.

_____

_____

_____

_____

_____

_____

_____

_____

How does it comfort you to know that God is _with us_ in the midst of our trials? When have you felt His presence in the midst of hard times?

_____

_____

_____

_____

_____

_____

_____

TWO
Imitating

Your Thirteen-Month-Old, Developmental Guide

Unexpected sloppy, wet kisses and total meltdowns—welcome to the joys and trials of toddlerhood. While people prepare you for the "terrible twos," no one really tells you what to expect with the wonderful and sometimes trying world of one-year-olds.

Your toddler is going through a world of transitions right now, and we all know transitions are hard. First, she is becoming more mobile. Whether or not your little one is walking yet, she certainly has more skills in the mobility department than just six short months ago. As her sights and desires shift further away from the play mat, frustration can arise when the corresponding coordination is not quite there. Continue to support her development and be patient if she's not walking yet. She's probably more frustrated than you are!

Speaking of frustration, communication is a difficult point right now for your little one, who understands much more than she can communicate. Most twelve-to-thirteen-month-olds have two to four words. Think about that for a moment. How hard would it be for you if you were limited to two to four words! So be patient with those meltdowns;

chances are your little one is trying to communicate something and growing frustrated.

If meltdowns are making you lose your mind, go through this simple acronym checklist: HALT. Ask yourself if your toddler is Hungry, Angry, Lonely, or Tired. Chances are the meltdown falls into one of these four categories. Try to get to the root of the problem, rather than just react to the emotion. This will help you stay calm and in control too.

Another transition your child may be going through is a caloric one. At this age your toddler is learning to get more of his calories from table food, but his appetites and tastes vary with the winds. A good rule of thumb is to offer him about one fourth of an adult portion and then let him choose what he wants to eat. Getting enough iron, fiber, and calcium is usually hard in the toddler years, so offer lots of choices high in these categories. Some breastfeeding moms will choose to wean around this time, while others will continue well into the year ahead. If you do wean or have been using formula, it's okay at this point to transition to cow's milk. Most doctors recommend whole milk until the child turns two and after that switching to a lower-fat concentration.

Finally, your little one's sleep patterns may be in transition. Most thirteen-month-olds need about eleven to fourteen hours of total sleep in a twenty-four-hour period and are still taking two naps at this age, but by about eighteen months may switch to one longer afternoon nap. If you notice getting your little one to sleep at night is suddenly becoming more challenging, or one of the two naps is becoming harder, it may be time to consolidate naps. You can experiment with putting her down for the morning nap a little later until soon she only needs that afternoon nap. Be patient; treating yourself and your little one with grace in these days of transition can go a long way toward making them sweet days and not frustrating ones.

Developmental Focus: Mimicry or Mirroring

Around the time of your baby's first birthday, you may notice a skill really beginning to take off: imitating others. Your toddler is beginning to watch and copy Mom or Dad with intentionality.

First, he may mimic because of the positive attention it garners. When you laugh and cheer with delight when your toddler does the touchdown dance like Daddy, guess what? He will likely do it again.

Second, she may imitate because of that feeling of bonding it brings. When she grabs her hairbrush when you grab yours, it may be because she is unconsciously seeking out that feeling of connection with you.

Third, imitation is one of the quickest ways to gain independence. As your toddler imitates your behaviors, she is learning how to do things on her own. And toddlers are hungry for independence.

Like all processes, imitation has its steps: watching and listening, processing the information, endeavoring to imitate, and practicing. As you can imagine, it's more important than ever to be a good role model at this stage; your little one is watching your every move. You'll also need to keep an eye out for ways that his imitation could put him in harm's way. Try to think like an imitating toddler as you take a look around your house, garage, and yard; this may help you make some important babyproofing changes that could prevent real harm to your little one.

This Month's Spiritual Focus: Imitating the Father and the Son

One of the grand themes in the Bible is imitating the Father. Like a toddler, we learn so much by imitating our God. This month we'll dive into all the ways the Bible invites us to pattern ourselves after His example as we grow to be more like Him.

Imitating the Father

"Truly, truly, I say to you, the Son can do nothing of his own accord, but only what he sees the Father doing. For whatever the Father does, that the Son does likewise."
JOHN 5:19 ESV

At the pool called Bethesda near the Sheep Gate in Jerusalem there was a man who had been lame for thirty-eight years. He lay there with a "multitude of invalids—blind, lame, and paralyzed" (John 5:3 ESV). It happened to be Shabbat, or Sabbath, when Jesus healed this lame man and commanded him to "Get up, take up your bed, and walk" (v. 8 ESV). And the Jewish leaders were ready to pounce.

In His defense, Jesus said He (the Son) only did what He saw His Father doing. Of course, this enraged the Jews all the more because Jesus called God His Father (v. 18 ESV). As we look this month at the subject of imitation, we start here because Jesus showed us what it is to be an imitator. He modeled for us imitating God. Here are things He shows us: First, we are to care more about God's approval than people's opinions. As the book of Colossians tells us, "And whatever you do, do it heartily, as to the Lord and not to men" (3:23). Second, He was not seeking human glory but God's (John 5:44 ESV). Finally, He modeled dependence on God: "I can do nothing on my own" (v. 30 ESV). Here our toddlers can be instructive to us. Take a minute to notice today how utterly dependent your toddler is on you. Instead of feeling annoyed by this, use moments throughout the day to offer up little prayers to God such as, "God, thank You for reminding me that I need You constantly, just as my toddler needs me." Jesus modeled God that we might model Him.

Teaching the Example of the Father

"But love your enemies, do good, and lend, hoping for nothing in return; and your reward will be great, and you will be sons of the Most High."
LUKE 6:35

There's hardly anything cuter than when your toddler does something in imitation of you. Maybe you crinkle your nose a bit when you smile, and so does your little one. Or perhaps it's the way you nod your head empathetically as you listen, and your toddler is already picking up the habit. Or perhaps it's Daddy's bear hugs that today your toddler is perfecting. In the previous devotion, we looked at how Jesus imitated His Father. Today, as we look at Jesus' most famous sermon, we notice that He not only models Himself after the Father but also teaches us to pattern ourselves after the Father.

After giving His listeners a very countercultural exhortation to love their enemies and bless those who curse them, Jesus pointed to God the Father and His behavior toward us as the ultimate example of this principle. Jesus draws our attention to how God exhibits this kind of mercy and largesse to us as our ultimate reason and motivation for showing this mercy to others. He also uses family bonds as a motivation, saying, "You will be sons of the Most High," if you imitate the Father in this way. In other words, people will notice your similarity to God, your likeness, in how you imitate Him. Children learn the father's business, and God's business is being merciful to those who need mercy. This is who He is.

Follow Me as I Follow Him

*"As the Father loved Me, I also have loved
you; abide in My love. If you keep My
commandments, you will abide in My love,
just as I have kept My Father's commandments
and abide in His love. These things I have
spoken to you, that My joy may remain
in you, and that your joy may be full."*
JOHN 15:9–11

Child psychologists say that one of the reasons little ones imitate their parents is for the bonding that occurs through it. If you are sipping from a straw and your little one picks up her sippy cup and sips at the same time, tilting her head to one side as you do yours, or if your husband likes to put his feet up in his favorite chair while he reads a book and your little one leans back next to him, stretched out with a board book, chances are your toddler is looking for connection. Unconsciously, he or she is craving that special bond that occurs through imitation.

As I read this passage in John 15, I can't help but think of the special bond between Jesus and the Father as He abides in the Father's love and keeps His commands. The eternal bond that Christ has known with the Father He wants to invite us to know also. As we abide in Jesus and His love—as we keep His commandments—we get to know this special bond. This is a bond of love and an intimacy that Jesus tells us will bring us fullness of joy. Isn't it interesting that Jesus tells us that the way to abide in His love is to keep His commandments? This isn't a kind of conditional love statement—if you do this, I'll love you—but rather it's an indication of the fact that God's commands are *for our good*. These are commands that keep us imitating God's heart, which keeps us from evil and its consequent suffering. Keeping His commandments is the way to imitate the Father's heart; it's the way to bond with Him and abide with Him. It's the toddler putting his feet up next to Dad with a picture book in hand. It's our way to be like Him.

Have you noticed your toddler imitating you or your spouse? What expressions or mannerisms have you noticed are already similar?

_____

_____

_____

_____

_____

Do you have trouble believing that God's commands are good for you, or is this quite easy for you to believe? Do you think that consciously seeking to imitate God might make you feel more bonded with Him?

_____

_____

_____

_____

God's Self-Portrait

In the past God spoke to our ancestors through the prophets . . . but in these last days he has spoken to us by his Son . . . the radiance of God's glory and the exact representation of his being."
HEBREWS 1:1–3 NIV

While your toddler isn't quite old enough yet to do much more than scribble, it won't be long before those scribbles will take on meaning and be gifted to you in love. As my toddlers have matured into preschoolers, so have those notes. I treasure the little hand-drawn stick figures representing my little guy, myself, and my husband with hearts of love all over the page. Even though the self-portrait is rudimentary, it still represents something real: the love that exists in his heart and in our family.

In Hebrews 1, God tells us that He also has painted a self-portrait and given it to us. What is His self-portrait? It is Jesus, His Son, "the exact representation of his being." We learn that God spoke over the ages, giving us glimpses into His nature. He spoke through the Law, through the wisdom literature (specifically the books of Psalms, Proverbs, Ecclesiastes, and Job), and through the prophets, but none of these could show Him to us quite like Jesus shows us the Father. God wanted us to have a personal relationship with Him, so only the person of His Son could communicate to us the depth of His desire to be *with us*. God paints Himself into our scene with Jesus, not in two dimensions, not in words alone. God's love is writ larger than any hand-drawn hearts. It is written in the arms of Jesus stretched wide on a cross, a living, breathing masterpiece of God's love on display for us to know and for us to imitate.

The Basin and the Towel

"If I then, your Lord and Teacher, have washed your feet, you also ought to wash one another's feet. For I have given you an example, that you should do as I have done to you."
JOHN 13:14–15

As we continue thinking about what it means to imitate God, we come to one of the most moving passages of Scripture. Here Jesus invites us to imitate Him in serving others. The chapter begins with, "When Jesus knew that His hour had come" (John 13:1). Jesus was about to go through the biggest spiritual, emotional, and physical ordeal of His life on the cross. If at any time one would be justified in taking a moment for oneself or asking for the care and service of others, it would be this moment. But instead, Jesus served as He washed the disciples' feet.

In a sense this is a mini-metaphor for His whole life. He has taken off His outer garment—the glory He had known in eternity—and lowered Himself to the form of a human (Philippians 2:6–8). He has spent His life "washing the feet" of His people: healing the blind, the lame, and the leprous, teaching and caring for their needs. And now through this symbolic act, the teacher gave one last lesson and asked His students (and, by extension, us) to emulate Him.

As mothers of little ones, we have ample opportunity to practice this call of service. We can do it begrudgingly or mindlessly, or we can serve in a spirit of worship as we do even the most menial tasks—changing diapers, cleaning high chair trays, or washing soiled sheets—as conscious acts of spiritual service and worship. As Paul urged us, "Whatever you do, do it heartily, as to the Lord and not to men" (Colossians 3:23). We can serve God even as we serve our toddlers and our families.

Mirror, Mirror

*But we all, with unveiled face, beholding as
in a mirror the glory of the Lord, are being
transformed into the same image from glory
to glory, just as by the Spirit of the Lord.*
2 CORINTHIANS 3:18

Has your toddler discovered herself in the mirror yet? If not, this is a fun time to introduce her to herself. You can have a good time making silly faces, pointing to eyes, ears, and mouth, or just placing her hands against the mirror for her to notice the movement as she moves her hands or body. While it may still be several months before your little one recognizes that the reflection in the mirror is her own, the learning and play opportunities abound. When you see it through your toddler's eyes, you may remember there is something wondrous about a mirror. But as fascinating as a normal mirror is to your toddler, we have a mirror yet more wondrous and instructive.

As we come to this passage in 2 Corinthians, Paul has been describing how Moses' face had to be covered with a veil after beholding God because his face was so radiant no one could look upon it. The Israelites' sin made God's glory unbearable to them. But then Paul said, "When one turns to the Lord, the veil is taken away" (v. 16). We look "with unveiled face, beholding as in a mirror the glory of the Lord." But unlike a normal mirror, we don't see ourselves; we see the perfect One. As we look into the Word, as we study the perfections of God, and as we admire and marvel at Him, by the Spirit something begins to happen to us. We begin to long to be like Him. God gives us a holy longing to be like the face of glory in the mirror. He helps us to crave goodness and gives us a distaste for sin. Little by little, as we cooperate with Him, He transforms us more and more into the likeness of Christ. Now this truly seems a fairy tale–like wonder, doesn't it? As we study His character and pray for His grace, and as we peer into this mirror, we don't see who we are but who, by His Spirit, we are becoming like.

If you could paint a picture of your toddler with words right now, how would you describe him or her? Whom does he or she favor? What little peeks into his or her personality are you seeing already?

_____

_____

_____

_____

_____

We've talked this week about imitating our servant Savior, Jesus. How can seeing our service as mothers of toddlers as "to the Lord" (Colossians 3:23) transform even the smallest tasks of mothering into spiritual acts of worship?

_____

_____

_____

_____

_____

_____

The Heart of Service

Do nothing from selfish ambition or conceit, but in humility count others more significant than yourselves. Let each of you look not only to his own interests, but also to the interests of others.
PHILIPPIANS 2:3–4 ESV

As we continue thinking about what it means to imitate Jesus, Paul asks us to look to Christ's example: "Who, though he was in the form of God, did not count equality with God a thing to be grasped, but emptied himself, by taking the form of a servant" (Philippians 2:6–7 ESV). Child psychologists name four parts of a child's act of imitation: observation, processing, practicing, and imitating.[2] Likewise, let us begin by observing. We see first that Christ was a servant. He was not a servant in outward appearance only. We, too, are to serve not out of rivalry or conceit. Sometimes we serve as a way to compete with others. Sometimes we serve out of pride, to feel a sense of superiority. We are instead invited to "in humility count others more significant" than ourselves.

We can also fall off the horse on the other side—with a martyr complex. But Paul protected against this error as well, saying we should look "not only to [our] own interests, but also to the interests of others." Inherent in this is a good reminder. Paul took for granted that we will naturally be concerned with our own interests. There must be some degree of self-care before we have the ability to care for others. But then we are to turn our attention outward, like Jesus.

The next step in this imitation process is to practice. Practice implies that we won't do it all right. We are going to mess up and need to observe, process, try, fail, and try again. But as we do, we will find our Christlike service becoming more reflexive and reflective of Jesus.

Mimic Me

Imitate me, just as I also imitate Christ.

1 CORINTHIANS 11:1

So far this month, as we've considered the biblical theme of imitating God, we've seen something of a progression. We've seen how Jesus imitated the Father, how He pointed to God as an example and model in His teaching for us to follow, and then how He encouraged us to imitate Him as He imitates God. Now as we come to the Epistles (Paul's letters to the churches), we see the apostles imitating Jesus, using Jesus as an example, and then calling us to imitate them as they imitate Christ.

In 1 Corinthians 11, Paul talked about how even though his conscience permitted him to do something, if it caused another to stumble, he would not do it. He'd rather sacrifice his own freedoms for the sake of bringing someone into the kingdom than keep his freedoms and cause someone to miss Jesus. And he encouraged us to do the same. Here we see a pattern. We are to live such upright lives in imitation of Christ that we can say with Paul, "Imitate me, just as I also imitate Christ." This should not be with the goal of puffing ourselves up with pride. Remember, our hearts matter. But we should be living such commendable lives that we are providing visible models to the world of what Jesus is like. We should be helping others see Jesus through us. This is a high but worthy goal.

To bring it home more, as you think about this passage in light of your calling as a mother, remember that before your child ever understands what it means to imitate God, he will understand what it means to imitate you.

Imitating Our Brothers and Sisters

*Brothers, join in imitating me, and keep
your eyes on those who walk according
to the example you have in us.*
PHILIPPIANS 3:17 ESV

As we continue thinking about what it means to imitate God, we've seen Christ imitate the Father and teach us to imitate them both. We've seen the apostles imitate Jesus and teach us to imitate Jesus and them. And now we see Paul encouraging us to imitate any Christian who is walking according to the example of Christ.

This is one of the reasons you and I need the fellowship of other believers. And it is why we need our families to be in the fellowship of a local church. We need to be surrounding ourselves and our children with other imitators of Christ.

None of us will imitate Christ perfectly. But some of our brothers and sisters will imitate Christ better in some areas than we do. Perhaps we need that older mother figure in Christ who has learned to be a patient and understanding mom to help us flesh that out in our own families. Or perhaps your husband needs that brother in Christ who models firm faith in the face of persecution. Or maybe your toddler needs to feel the joy of Christians singing praises to God together in unison. God gives us these living examples to help us grow in our likeness to Him.

But Paul told us in the same passage to be on guard: "For many, of whom I have often told you and now tell you even with tears, walk as enemies of the cross of Christ" (v. 18 ESV). In other words, we need to exercise discernment. Not everyone—even in the church—is a true believer and worthy of our imitation. So yes, we are invited to imitate other believers who walk according to Christ's example, but we need to be cautious and discern who is a true example worthy of our imitation.

This past week with your toddler was full of ups and downs, I'm sure. As I encouraged you in the introduction, it won't all be perfect moments, but we can find beauty in the moments we have and treasure them. What ordinary moments of joy with your little one do you want to remember from this week?

_____

_____

_____

_____

Who has God placed in your life that is worthy of imitation in one way or another? What aspects of godliness do you see in them that you are emulating or that you consider worthy of imitation?

_____

_____

_____

_____

_____

A Household of Imitators

Therefore be imitators of God as dear children.
EPHESIANS 5:1

Context is king. As we continue to focus this month on what it means to imitate God, I want us to think about how this plays out in our homes. Here in the book of Ephesians, we have one of the most detailed treatments of the dynamics of family life in the New Testament. But it's all about context. Everything that Paul said to husbands, everything he said to wives and to children, was in the context of this verse: "Therefore be imitators of God as dear children." The "therefore" at the beginning of this verse directs us back to the point Paul had just made about the character of our God. He wrote, "Be kind to one another, tenderhearted, forgiving one another, as God in Christ forgave you" (4:32 ESV). God sets the example of kindness and forgiveness for us to imitate as dearly loved children.

As we imitate God in this, we are to live out our marriages as such robust models of the love of God that our children and others see a living picture of the love of Christ in how we love and sacrifice and submit to one another.

Many of you who are reading this book are at the very start of your journey of child-rearing and discipline. What a great time to work on the context of this verse. What a great time to consider the kindness and tenderhearted forgiveness of Christ toward you and imitate those in your love for your spouse. What a great time to work on becoming a model worthy of emulation, laying the groundwork and context out of which you lovingly call your children to obedience.

A Work in Progress

*Not that I have already obtained this
or am already perfect, but I press on
to make it my own, because Christ
Jesus has made me his own.*
PHILIPPIANS 3:12 ESV

As parents we want to model Christ for our children. We want to be faithful imitators such that our children have an example worthy of following. But we know we are not there yet. None of us are perfect examples. None of us ever will be perfect examples on this side of eternity. We are flawed. We fail and we will fail our children. But this isn't an excuse. A few verses after these, where Paul described his imperfect progress, he called the Philippians to "join in imitating me" (v. 17 ESV). But wait! He just said he's a work in progress, right? Exactly!

Guess what? The Christian life is a journey of sanctification, of growing more and more in our likeness to Christ. Our children need examples of what it looks like to be striving toward that goal. They need to see what godliness looks like even in failure. (It looks like repentance and faith.) We confess our failures and flee to Christ in faith, knowing He has already died for all our sins. And we exercise faith once more to keep on straining toward the goal—toward the "prize of the upward call of God in Christ Jesus." This is the model Paul gave—not a perfect model, but an in-progress model. And this is the model he called us to likewise imitate. We can point our children to ourselves even as we point them to Christ as their ultimate model and example.

A Relay Race

*You know what kind of men we proved to be
among you for your sake. And you became
imitators of us and of the Lord, for you received
the word in much affliction, with the joy of the
Holy Spirit, so that you became an example to
all the believers in Macedonia and in Achaia.*
1 THESSALONIANS 1:5–7 ESV

The Christian life—and especially the Christian parenting life—is a bit like a relay race. In this passage, we see the pattern of mature believers imitating Christ and pouring their lives out for their spiritual children. We see the children growing up into maturity and becoming an example to even more. The beauty of their imitation of Christ "has gone forth everywhere, so that we need not say anything" (1 Thessalonians 1:8 ESV). Imagine pouring your heart into shaping your little one into a disciple of Christ such that one day he or she is such a vibrant example of faith that when you go to your grown child's town you don't need to teach anyone the gospel because they've already seen and heard it through your son or daughter. Imagine how breathtaking that would be!

But here's the backstory. Let me warn you, it is a labor of love. Paul reminded the Thessalonians of how he and his fellow travelers served the Thessalonians: "But we were gentle among you, like a nursing mother taking care of her own children. So, being affectionately desirous of you, we were ready to share with you not only the gospel of God but also our own selves" (2:7–8 ESV).

How did these mature Thessalonian believers come about? They were created through Paul's poured-out life—through the giving of his very self. He went on: "You remember, brothers, our labor . . . night and day," and, "You know how, like a father with his children, we exhorted each one of you and encouraged you and charged you to walk in a manner worthy of God" (vv. 2:9, 11–12 ESV). So here it is, Mamas. This journey of bringing up imitators of Christ is a journey of pouring ourselves out over the long haul with the hope that one day our children will likewise pour themselves out for the sake of the gospel: passing the baton from one generation to the next.

What new skill or activity has your child mastered or enjoyed this week?

_____

_____

_____

_____

_____

Write a prayer for your son or daughter to grow up into a mature believer who also pours out his or her life to shape Christ in others.

_____

_____

_____

_____

_____

_____

_____

THREE
Resting

Your Fourteen-Month-Old,

Developmental Guide

Your little one may be a bundle of energy these days—and a bundle of contradictions! This is the age of burgeoning independence and also burgeoning separation anxiety. That means one moment your toddler may be pushing you away while he tries something for himself and the next minute crying when he sees you leaving the room. Don't worry; that's all a part of toddlerhood. It's a great thing that your little one is working on his independence. That means he's trying new things, wanting to learn, and forming his own sense of identity apart from you! And the fact that he's nervous when you leave is a sign that he's attached to you—and that's a good thing. The best thing you can do is stay calm and make your exit reassuring, positive, and fairly quick if possible.

If your toddler is having trouble sharing, not to fear—this is normal too. You'll be working on this one for a while. Be patient. Distract him with a different toy when you can. And understand that the older your little one gets, the easier concepts like "you can get it back soon" will make sense to him. In the meantime, don't lament that you've failed the parenting game just because your child is having a hard time sharing with a friend or sibling. You haven't. Learning to share you or a toy takes time.

You might also be despairing if your toddler is a picky eater these days. But actually, being choosy with foods is quite normal at this age. Pediatricians know that toddler appetites and tastes are challenging, to say the least. Instead of daily nutritional goals, try to think in terms of an entire week with a toddler and see that she is getting a variety of fruits, veggies, fiber, iron, and calcium-rich foods over the course of the week and not just over the course of the day. This helps alleviate some mealtime stress. Also, if the only way your toddler will eat veggies is pureed as baby food or the only way she'll eat ground beef is hidden in her yogurt, don't feel bad about getting the nutrients in incognito.

Your little one is not all fuss, however. She's also growing in a lot of important skills. If she's been walking for a while, you'll notice her confidence really starting to soar. She may be able to balance as she stops to pick something up, or you may find her trying new skills that require more coordination. If your toddler still isn't there yet, never fear; normal walking age varies from nine to eighteen months.

Another skill your toddler is developing is hand-eye coordination. You've noticed she's better at getting the food to her mouth or maybe holding a spoon, but how can you help your little one improve hand-eye coordination even more? Stacking blocks is a great activity for working on this, as is simply rolling a ball back and forth or tossing a beanbag or other soft ball back and forth.

Developmental Focus: Rest

Sleep! Ah, glorious sleep! Rest is really important to your toddler's brain growth, believe it or not. All those good things they are learning during the day are cemented during naps or the night's rest, so making sure your little one gets ample sleep is a top priority in these busy days of toddler life.

Pediatricians recommend eleven to fourteen hours of total sleep in a twenty-four-hour period. This might be broken up with two one-hour daytime naps (morning and afternoon) and nighttime rest lasting eleven to twelve hours, or your toddler might be starting to move to one longer nap. When you notice him edging toward this transition or having difficulty getting to bed at night, you can try moving the morning nap slightly later day by day until he is just taking the one longer nap in the afternoon.

Also, sleep regression is common around this age. If night-waking is happening, one thing you can try (which seems counterintuitive) is moving bedtime earlier. When a child goes from tired to overtired, her brain can become hyperstimulated, which can actually make it more difficult to fall asleep and stay asleep.

Establishing a nighttime routine of winding down is also helpful. Rocking and reading picture books are great ways to close your day together. Singing a hymn or praise song and praying together are also really beautiful habits to begin. However you find yourself closing the day, your toddler will most likely thrive on predictability.

One thing to keep an eye out for: as your toddler learns to stand and walk, learning to climb isn't far behind. If he is starting to climb out of his crib, make sure you've put the crib on its lowest setting. Most kids won't physically be able to climb out of the crib until about eighteen to twenty-four months, but if your little Spider-Man is on the early side, you may have to transition to a toddler bed. The big challenge once you transition is teaching him to stay in the bed, so if he is not climbing out yet, you may want to leave well enough alone. You may also need the crib for another baby. If this is the case, try to make the bed transition a few months before or after baby's arrival. That way you are not piling two major transitions on top of the other. You don't want your toddler to feel displaced.

This Month's Spiritual Focus: Resting in Jesus

Rest is such a beautiful and repeated theme in the Scriptures. How we long for it, and how we need it! Yet, just like your toddler, you may fight God's invitation to rest. Learning to slow down and rest according to His rhythm can make all the difference in our spiritual and personal well-being, not just for you but for future generations. Rest and its far-reaching impact are so much bigger and more important than we think.

An Invitation for the Weary

"Come to Me, all you who labor and are heavy laden, and I will give you rest. Take My yoke upon you and learn from Me, for I am gentle and lowly in heart, and you will find rest for your souls."
MATTHEW 11:28–29

If there is anyone who knows weary, it is us mamas. But just because we are exhausted as mothers doesn't mean that we've learned to rest well or that we are champion invitation-accepters.

So what is holding us back from accepting Jesus' invitation to come to Him? Sometimes it's pride. We honestly believe that we have what it takes inside us to do it all, to be it all, that we are superwomen beyond the need of mere mortal trifles like sleep and downtime and spiritual nourishment.

But other times, it's because we don't really know our God. What's your view of God? Ask your heart in an unguarded moment: How do you really feel about God? Is He harsh and demanding? Is He criticizing, shaking His head in disappointment at your failures? Is He always expecting more, better, faster?

Or do you have the view of God (not only in your head, but in the deepest places of your heart) that we see here in this passage. Do you know—really know—that your God is gentle with you? That He humbly beckons you to rest—rest from your worries, from your cares, from your own impossible expectations, from your strivings for things that in the end do not matter and do not satisfy? If you don't deeply know God as this gentle giver, I pray that knowledge would make its way today from your head to your heart.

He Gently Leads

He tends his flock like a shepherd: he gathers
the lambs in his arms and carries them close to
his heart; he gently leads those that have young.

ISAIAH 40:11 NIV

Our God is a gentle shepherd. As we continue thinking about this theme of rest and how God is gentle with us, I couldn't help but think of this verse. Our God knows what an exhausting, demanding job we have as mothers. He made every minuscule part of the design of mothers and children, and He walks intimately with us through motherhood. He is not a harsh and demanding shepherd who beats the ewes with their baby lambs because of failure to keep up with the rest. "'I will feed My flock, and I will make them lie down,' says the Lord GOD" (Ezekiel 34:15). No, He gathers the weak and the tired in His arms. He carries the lambs close to His heart.

Do you need God to make you lie down? I know I'm guilty of being a go-go-go type of Martha sometimes (Luke 10:38–42). And sometimes, especially in these tiring days with little ones, I need God to *make* me lie down, like He does with His sheep. "He makes me to lie down in green pastures; He leads me beside the still waters. He restores my soul," said David (Psalm 23:2–3). God cares about your body, how tired you are, how worn out. And He cares about your soul, how spiritually thirsty you are as you give and give and give. When it comes to the spiritual life, like a nursing ewe, you are eating for two. God sees. He knows. He cares. He is gentle with you, Mama, and wants to give you rest. He invites you to lay even the burden of your precious lamb in His arms. He will carry your little one close to His heart.

47

He Provides Rest
for Mothers

*When Jesus therefore saw His mother, and the
disciple whom He loved standing by, He said to His
mother, "Woman, behold your son!" Then He said
to the disciple, "Behold your mother!" And from
that hour that disciple took her to his own home.*
JOHN 19:26–27

I know this may be a strange verse to plop down in the middle of a
study on rest, but I believe this is a word that some women today need to
hear. Being a mother is a vulnerable role. The act of bringing a life into
this world and then sustaining and caring for that life is an act that in
a physical and even a financial sense makes us vulnerable. Many, if not
most, women who choose to be moms do so at a cost to their careers, to
their bodies, and to their finances. I don't say this to diminish the blessings
of motherhood—which are huge and well worth it—but to acknowledge
that as women, motherhood makes us more vulnerable. Ideally, a loving
marriage is the context into which a child comes into this world, with
two parents to sustain this blessed burden, both the financial cost and the
spiritual labor of it. But many times, because of either death or divorce, a
woman ends up laboring under this burden alone.

What I hear in some of what were the very last words of Jesus on the
cross—in the middle of His own agony—is Jesus' care and concern for
His mother, but also, by extension, mothers everywhere. Elsewhere in the
book of Isaiah, God reminds us, "Even to your old age and gray hairs I am
he, I am he who will sustain you. I have made you and I will carry you;
I will sustain you and I will rescue you" (Isaiah 46:4 NIV). I'm not sure

what particular stresses or worries you are facing today. Some who read this will be struggling with the difficulties of single motherhood, others may even be facing their marriages crumbling, and some may be dealing with difficult financial decisions. Whatever you are facing, I hope you'll hear in Jesus' words a continuation of that call for you to rest in Him. He will care for you and your little one. He will sustain you. He loves you.

Cultivating the gift of presence with your little one is so important. Make a habit of disconnecting from everything else and tuning in to your little one. When you do, what aspects of your toddler do you most enjoy? What brings a smile to your face?

_____

_____

_____

_____

I hope you've seen the gentle heart of God toward you as a mom in the passages we've looked at this week. What has particularly spoken to you this week? Is there some way God is calling you to rest in Him today?

_____

_____

_____

_____

_____

Jesus Needed Rest

*Because so many people were coming and going
that they did not even have a chance to eat,
[Jesus] said to [his disciples], "Come with me by
yourselves to a quiet place and get some rest."*
MARK 6:31 NIV

Sometimes we can have a supermom complex. Somehow we think we
can do it all and not get burned out. Here's the thing: it's not the good
things that burn us out. It's the lack of rest that burns us out. Even Jesus,
Savior of the world, needed rest. Consider for a moment how short in the
scheme of things His time for public ministry truly was. He ministered
for three years before His death and resurrection. That's a little over one
thousand days. He knew His time was short, and yet He rested.

He trusted God to do what He needed to do through Him in that
limited time. He trusted that He could rest and leave the rest to God's
sovereign care. He showed the discipline to stop and care for His physical
needs and the needs of His ragtag crew. Guess what? You can too.

Do you need to get away by yourself for an hour or two, a day, or a
night? Pray about it; then ask for some help to make that a reality. Or
maybe you are someone who is recharged by time *with* people. Maybe
you need to give yourself permission to go out with the girls while your
spouse or babysitter watches the little one. Or to have a date night alone
with your spouse. Or maybe you need to put some playdates with a mama
friend on the calendar that are more for you than your toddler. That's
okay too.

Rest is necessary. Rest is a discipline. Rest recharges us for ministry.
Jesus rested, and so should you.

Too Busy Not to Pray

Very early in the morning, while it was still
dark, Jesus got up, left the house and went
off to a solitary place, where he prayed.
MARK 1:35 NIV

When my oldest was seven, I gave birth to our fifth son. I had lots of very little people pressing in on me, needing Mommy all the time. Some nights my arms ached just from holding children all day. I needed physical rest a lot during that time, but I also needed rest for my spirit. Thankfully, not only did Jesus model seeking physical rest for us, He modeled seeking spiritual rest in the midst of pressing demands.

Sometimes we need rest for our spirits more than we need anything else. Jesus repeatedly modeled withdrawing to pray. Luke recorded, "Yet the news about him spread all the more, so that crowds of people came to hear him and to be healed of their sicknesses. But Jesus often withdrew to lonely places and prayed" (Luke 5:15–16 NIV). Or as Matthew recorded, "After he had dismissed them, he went up on a mountainside by himself to pray. Later that night, he was [still] there alone" (Matthew 14:23 NIV).

When we are continually giving of ourselves, that's when we need time to be filled up more than ever. We need time for God to meet our needs and care for our concerns. We need to be filled up again to *want* to give of ourselves once more. We are too busy not to pray; too needed not to take time to be filled.

If you are there today, friend, I urge you to follow Jesus' example. Even if it's five minutes in your room praying, or finding a babysitter so you can go to a coffee shop alone with your Bible, do it. Your family needs what you have to give, but you won't have it unless you are receiving from God by experiencing His love and care for your soul.

51

Trusting in God's Enough

In vain you rise early and stay up late, toiling for food to eat—for he grants sleep to those he loves.
PSALM 127:2 NIV

We live in a culture of constant busy. If you listen closely to how people talk about their lives, you may hear a subtle glorification of the overworked, as if busy equates with value and importance. There is a balance in the Christian life. God does call us to seize the day: "So then, be careful how you walk, not as unwise people but as wise, making the most of your time, because the days are evil" (Ephesians 5:15–16 NASB 1995). He warns us against laziness: "A little sleep, a little slumber, a little folding of the hands to sleep—so shall your poverty come on you like a prowler" (Proverbs 6:10–11). But there is also the tendency to think it *all* depends on us: to fail to trust in God's provision, to work for excess instead of enough, to work to impress or to create material lust in our neighbor. These are clearly not of God.

This verse in Psalms is not intended for the lazy. It is a corrective for the heart that is not trusting. It dovetails with Jesus' words in the Sermon on the Mount to observe the birds of the air and the flowers of the field and how God cares for them—and to not be anxious (Matthew 6:25–36). The limits of our twenty-four-hour day, of our body's need for adequate sleep, are good tests of where our idols are. *If you don't have time for it all, maybe it's because you weren't called to it all.*

Today's verse is a call to examine our heart for idols. Even good things can become gods when pursued in excess. Your desire for a clean house, a perfect body, a successful home business, a little entertainment, or a showcase home can keep you up in vain. If you are exhausted, ask yourself why. Sometimes it is out of our control—the night-waking of a toddler, for instance. But other times our exhaustion reveals places where our hearts need correcting. Pray that God would help you discern the difference.

What bedtime rituals do you and your little one have these days? What sweet parts of the bedtime routine do you treasure?

_____

_____

_____

_____

_____

_____

What do you enjoy doing when you have downtime?

_____

_____

_____

_____

_____

_____

_____

_____

A God-Ordained Rhythm of Rest

*Then God blessed the seventh day and
sanctified it, because in it He rested from all
His work which God had created and made.*
GENESIS 2:3

I magine a day of rest—a day set apart for the renewing of the deepest parts of you: your soul, your imagination, your passion, and your relationships. Imagine God creating such a day and setting it apart, not as a burden for a busy mama to shoulder but as a blessing—as a gift. He did. Even though our God does not need rest, He made this special day and sanctified it for us. "The Sabbath was made for man, and not man for the Sabbath," says Jesus (Mark 2:27). Are you taking advantage of this God-given gift in these days of mothering a toddler? If the answer is no or not fully, I want to challenge you to stop and pray right now. Ask God to help you make some small but significant changes to reorient your life around this God-ordained rhythm of renewal.

I will not offer you a prescription for this day, but I will offer you some thoughts on important aspects of rest. First, our souls need rest. Gathering together to worship and fellowship with other believers is important. Do "not [give] up meeting together, as some are in the habit of doing" (Hebrews 10:25 NIV). Next, our bodies, our spirits, our minds need rest. Rest for you may not look like rest for me. For some, rest will be creative, for some it will be quiet, for others it might be exuberant and noisy. For all of us, especially parents of needy toddlers, rest will be imperfect. Yet even imperfect rest is better than no rest. Ask God to help you prioritize Sabbath rest.

Reorienting Your Life Around Sabbath

*'Tomorrow is a Sabbath rest, a holy Sabbath to
the LORD. Bake what you will bake today, and
boil what you will boil; and lay up for yourselves
all that remains, to be kept until morning.'*

EXODUS 16:23

When I was in college, I spent a summer with missionaries in Bogotá, Colombia. I really enjoyed watching how their young family with a toddler practiced Sabbath. On the Saturday before, they would cook enough for that night and also for a picnic-style meal to take to church. Other church families did the same. After church each Sunday, the congregation lingered together for a joyful lunch on the grounds. All the work had been done the night before, so there was ample time for fellowship and laughter. On Sunday evenings, after a nap for the toddler, the missionaries had a practice of a very simple meal: they invited a different member of the youth group over each week for pancakes. It was fun getting to know one teen at a time, and the hospitality never felt burdensome. Their lives oriented around Sabbath in a joyful, easy way.

In Jewish homes Sabbath, or Shabbat, is welcomed like an honored guest. Before it starts, the house is cleaned, people wash and dress in their best, and a wonderful meal is prepared. Everything is ready by sunset on Friday night. The wife lights a candle, and blessings are said. While Sabbath is a day of prayer, it is also a day of leisurely feasting and enjoyment. I share these ideas not as legalistic requirements but because these ideas have stoked my imagination to see how a little bit of pre-planning can help make Sabbath (even for moms) a day of true rest. Some planning and the right mindset can make it an anticipated apex of the week.

Sleep, Sabbath, Grace, and Trust

Remember that you were a slave in the land of Egypt, and the LORD your God brought you out from there by a mighty hand and by an outstretched arm; therefore the LORD your God commanded you to keep the Sabbath day.
DEUTERONOMY 5:15

You can find the Ten Commandments in their entirety in the Bible in two places: in Exodus 20:2–17 and in Deuteronomy 5:6–21. In the book of Exodus, the details concerning our "why" of Sabbath-keeping point back to how God rested on the seventh day of creation (Exodus 20:11). But the second time we are given the commandments, God shows that He also wants His people to remember their slavery in Egypt (Deuteronomy 5:15). What does keeping Sabbath have to do with enslavement in Egypt? For nearly four hundred years the Israelites were enslaved in Egypt. They did not get to rest even one day a week! No other culture or civilization had a practice of weekly rest. Sabbath was a picture of grace, of freedom from the things that enslave us, of jubilee. It points ahead to the exodus that Christ will lead us through—our exodus from sin. Jesus did what we could not do for ourselves. He freed us. As we keep the Sabbath in a postresurrection world, we remind ourselves of an eternal grace to come.

We have both daily and weekly reminders of this grace. You may have never thought of it this way, but each time we go to sleep, we rest in God's ability to handle our problems, our cares, even our vulnerable bodies. Sleep is a picture of grace, of God caring for us when we are unable to care for ourselves. Likewise, Sabbath is a resting from our labor, and it is a picture of God caring for our needs during our cessation from work. Our nightly rest and our weekly Sabbath are both declarations of trust that the God who made and sustains the universe is able to sustain us. And in this way they are healthy correctives for us. When some work is plaguing us so much we can't leave it alone for just one day a week, it might be a sign that it is an idol in our lives. And here's the amazing thing: keeping this Sabbath of rest holy to the Lord actually recharges and reinvigorates us for every other day of the week.

Does your little one have any special loveys, stuffed animals, or blankets to which he or she has developed an attachment? Where and how does your little one rest best these days?

_____

_____

_____

_____

What are some things you particularly enjoy doing on your day of rest?

_____

_____

_____

_____

_____

Rest from Our Anxiety

Be anxious for nothing, but in everything by prayer and supplication, with thanksgiving, let your requests be made known to God; and the peace of God, which surpasses all understanding, will guard your hearts and minds through Christ Jesus.
PHILIPPIANS 4:6–7

All of us experience anxiety. How comforting to know that Jesus cares about it and gives us specifics on how to combat it. As anxious thoughts arise, we are to take them captive (2 Corinthians 10:5). We should see each anxious thought not as a hamster wheel to go around on but rather a conversation starter with our Father who loves us and cares about us. We take each of these anxieties to God in prayer. Notice how as Paul talked about it, he moved from prayer in a general sense to petition, which is a specific request, to thanksgiving, which is a particular prayer of gratitude. That's because we have a God who meets us in our anxiety, who cares for us in our fears, and who can alleviate them with His presence. As we bring our anxiety to Him, the peace of God stands guard in our hearts and minds against distortions of truth.

Even with bouts of normal anxiety, we all need help from time to time. But when our anxiety is off the charts, our needs for outside help are even greater. Before I leave this topic of dealing with what is normal for everyone, it is important to mention that postpartum anxiety is an often-overlooked disorder that affects about 10 percent of mothers. If you are feeling excessive anxiety, please get help from your doctor and a counselor. Don't let this rob you of peace. There's no shame in getting the help you need.

Rest in His Power

*A furious squall came up, and the waves broke
over the boat, so that it was nearly swamped.
Jesus was in the stern, sleeping on a cushion.*

MARK 4:37–38 NIV

I love this story from the book of Mark. Jesus was exhausted. He had just finished teaching some of His most memorable parables from a boat on a lake because of the enormity of the crowds. He taught all day, until He was so exhausted that He asked the disciples to take Him to the other side of the lake, just to get a break. He'd fallen asleep when an enormous squall came up. Waves were breaking left and right, threatening to overwhelm the vessel while Jesus slept. His disciples roused Him, pleading, "Teacher, don't you care if we drown?" (Mark 4:38 NIV). But Jesus simply rebuked the winds and the waves as if they were a couple of household pets that had gotten out of hand when the guests arrived, saying, "Quiet. Be still!" (v. 39 NIV). And the storm lay down like a pacified dog with a new chew toy.

The message: God's got this. Look how Jesus can rest in the storm. He knew it was coming. Yet He could sleep because His Father was in absolute control. His Father made the wind, the waves, the rain, even the gravitational pull of the moon that rules the tides and high-pressure zones that cause the tempest. He made the storm, He controls it, and Jesus can rest because He rests in God's absolute authority over every iota of this world. Jesus is a picture of calm because He is a picture of trust in God's goodness and power. Mama, where do you need to remember today that there is not one particle of this world that is outside of the control of our loving God? As you give to that growing toddler and look toward the years ahead, remember Jesus cares and, yes, He can rest and you can rest, too, because God is powerful and good. He's got this.

Rest in This Moment

Therefore do not worry about tomorrow, for tomorrow will worry about its own things. Sufficient for the day is its own trouble.
MATTHEW 6:34

I don't know about you, but I can drive myself crazy with what-ifs. In a matter of minutes, I can create a Choose-My-Own-Adventure novel of my future with each ending worse than the one before. This isn't what God wants for us. It's ugly and it robs us of the goodness God has for us in this present moment. Jesus speaks against the endless disturbance of worry in our lives in His famous Sermon on the Mount. He called us to look up and see the birds of the air, to look around and see the flowers of the field. Can you feel the peace in this invitation? Can you feel the pull back to the present moment—back to the immediacy of the sight and sound of that bird on the wing flying by, back to the smell and the feel of the field of flowers at hand? It's an invitation to the present—an invitation to *be* present.

I think as mothers we especially need this invitation. How easy it is to get five or ten steps ahead worrying. From missed childhood milestones to preoccupations with future ones, we miss out on the wonder and joy of the present moment with this miracle of life right before our eyes. We miss out on another moment of ordinary extraordinary with our spouse. We miss out on the wonder of the fluttering bird outside, the waving field of flowers, or whatever wonders Jesus has given us this very day, if we only had eyes to see. Yes, each day has trouble of its own, but isn't it easier to take this day's trouble to God and petition Him for His help than to take the potential trouble of the next five or ten years to Him? I think that's what Jesus is getting at. God alone can see the future. But He calls us to live without such knowledge. Maybe it's time to trust that this is for the best.

What ordinary extraordinary moment do you want to remember from this week with your little one? What little aspect of your toddler do you want to slow down and enjoy in the week to come?

_____

_____

_____

_____

_____

_____

We've talked this week about taking anxious thoughts captive with prayer, remembering the power of God in our storms, and being present in the moment. Which of these lessons particularly struck you as something you need to practice more?

_____

_____

_____

_____

_____

_____

_____

FOUR
Washing

Your Fifteen-Month-Old,

Developmental Guide

When it comes to your fifteen-month-old, there are lots of reasons to cheer. By now, your little gal may be learning to stack blocks or cups to make a tower. And she may now finally be starting to master the quintessential baby toy: the shape sorter! Peekaboo? Check. She's nailed that game too. Whatever her little victories, make sure you are taking the time to stop and cheer her on. Let her know you delight in her little delights (and feel the angst of her frustrations).

Her successes come with lots of messes though, don't they? She's learning to use a cup! Yay! But then she also learns the orange juice is fun to pour, and she sloshes it into the Cheerios and off the high chair. She's learning to use a spoon. Hooray! But oops, she just learned it is fun to drop it when it's full of little green peas and watch Mom pick them up. Not-so-hooray. Unfortunately, the learning and the mess go hand in hand.

But it's not just high-chair time that's exhausting; your little one is likely maturing from those first awkward steps to an ability to dart down the hall or up the steps. Keeping ahead of her is no easy task, especially on the playground. (Mama, if you are having to do contortions you didn't know you could do to guide her up the playground steps and down through that kiddie slide, you are not alone. These things were not made for the adults who are trying to keep up with wobbly toddlers!)

Hopefully you aren't the only one wearing out at the playground. At this age your child is likely sleeping twelve to fourteen hours a day and still taking two naps, but you may see signs that those days are changing. Some days he may skip the morning nap and fall apart at the playdate (don't let those tantrums embarrass you, Mom; we mamas have been there!). Other days he may sleep too long during that morning nap and skip the afternoon one entirely. (Isn't dinner a delight on those nights? Hardly!) These are the days when mamas learn flexibility. And we also must learn to handle a good old tantrum.

When the inevitable meltdown occurs, remind yourself to HALT, and ask yourself if your child might be Hungry, Angry, Lonely, or Tired. Nine times out of ten, your little one is melting down for one of these four reasons. Stopping to address these key issues can often make the other issue go away.

These are the days of celebrations and fits. May God give you the grace and sense of humor to take it all in stride. The sweet moments and the hard ones come in such a precious little package. Hold on to the good at the end of the day, and let go of the rough stuff. God will see you both through it.

Practical Focus: Bathing

Bath time for toddlers: they either love it or hate it, don't they? A lot will depend on your child's personality. For some little ones, bath time is the favorite time of day, while others may be terrified of the water or possibly the drain. Either way, a daily bath is not a must. Some parents choose it because it is a great daily calming ritual, especially before bedtime. But if your schedule or your toddler's personality doesn't make that a good fit, don't sweat it. Bathing two to three times a week is generally enough to keep a toddler clean, especially if you have a daily habit of at least washing their face and genital area.

Bath-time safety is still a big concern. While you may have ditched the baby tub, you can't ditch the bath-time safety rules. Here are a few important things to keep in mind:

- Never leave your toddler unattended in the tub.
- Gather everything you will need for bath time before you turn on the water.
- If something comes up and you need to answer a phone call or the front door, solve a sibling meltdown, etc., get your little one safely out of the tub first!
- Always drain the tub when not in use and remove the plug.
- Nonslip mats in the tub or shower can help prevent falls.
- Fill the tub no higher than your toddler's belly button when seated.
- Make sure the water temperature is below 100 degrees F. Most children prefer the temperature cooler than their parents do.
- Check your water-heater settings. (It takes just two seconds for a child to receive third-degree burns from water that is 150 degrees F, and five seconds if it is 140 degrees F, which is often the factory setting on hot-water heaters.)

If your little one is afraid of the water, here are some things you can try:

- Let your little one pick out some bath toys: rubber ducks, boats, waterproof books, bath paints, or crayons. Sometimes just bringing the fun is all it takes.
- Some children are afraid of the drain. If so, let your child exit the tub and even the room before draining.
- Some kids are more comfortable in the bathtub with their swimsuit on at first. Not a problem.

This Month's Spiritual Focus: Being Washed

The Bible often employs the metaphor of washing or cleansing when it talks about our relationship with sin. This month we'll explore the various ways God uses the metaphor of cleansing and what it means for us as we grow in sanctification and grace.

A Cleansing Call to Repentance

"Wash yourselves, make yourselves clean; put away the evil of your doings from before My eyes."
ISAIAH 1:16

A friend of mine recently told me the harrowing story of her son's adoption from the Congo. After years of bureaucratic red tape and slowdowns from inner turmoil in the country, they managed to get her three-year-old son out of a desperate situation. When he came to them in Kenya, she remembers how he and the caregiver transporting him reeked of vomit, urine, and excrement. Their escape had been tumultuous, their route dangerous. That evening, as she bathed her son for the first time, was a significant moment of transformation. Her son has had many baths and showers since then, but this first bath under her care was significant and symbolic—a transfer from his old life to his new.

The Bible uses the cleansing metaphor when it talks about our regeneration. This is an initial but significant cleansing. It doesn't mean that we will never be muddied by sin again, but like that bath on the evening my friend received her newly adopted son, it was a turning point, and a major one. Passages like this should provoke us to great thanksgiving. While we were in the filth of our sin, God called us, rescued us, adopted us, and cleansed us. Next time you see your toddler covered in grime and needing a bath, praise God that He did not leave us as we were but has cleansed us through regeneration and continues to cleanse us through sanctification.

Whiter than Snow

*"Though your sins are like scarlet, they
shall be as white as snow; though they are
red like crimson, they shall be as wool."*
ISAIAH 1:18

My fourth-grade science fair project was a sign of things to come for me: I tested leading brands of laundry detergent to find the most effective stain remover for grass, chocolate pudding, grape jelly, and red ink. Little did I know then how much laundry I was destined for in the future as a mom to six boys! I don't remember the winning detergent, but I do remember nothing could remove the stains completely. Once the cloth was stained, it never looked new again.

God's cleansing work through Jesus in regeneration is of a different sort. In Jesus, we are washed, sanctified, and justified (1 Corinthians 6:11). Our cleansing in Christ is a revolutionary one. Without Christ, "all our righteousnesses are like filthy rags" (Isaiah 64:6). That means our best works (not our worst) before we came to know Him are like filthy rags. But when Christ regenerates and cleanses us, He no longer sees us stained. He sees us cleansed like the purest white, freshly fallen snow.

The word *amnesty* is the same word from which we derive the word *amnesia*, or total forgetfulness. In Christ, we have amnesty. Mamas, your view of yourself affects how you interact with your toddler. You can parent from a place of calm, knowing you are secure in Christ. You don't have to prove anything or earn His favor. He loves you; He's covered you in His righteousness. Toddler meltdowns can't soil your robes. Golden toddler behavior won't win you a crown. Jesus has dressed you in His perfect robes of righteousness.

67

Washed in Grace
to Give Grace

*Not by works of righteousness which we have
done, but according to His mercy He saved
us, through the washing of regeneration
and renewing of the Holy Spirit.*
TITUS 3:5

Before Paul talked about the cleansing of regeneration, he also talked about what kinds of people we were before that cleansing. In Titus 3, he reminded his hearers that they were "once foolish, disobedient, led astray, slaves to various passions and pleasures, passing our days in malice and envy, hated by others and hating one another" (Titus 3:3 ESV). He followed a similar pattern when he discussed the washing of regeneration in 1 Corinthians 6:9–11. He first reminded them of who they were and then reminded them of what God had done. Why?

Paul wanted us to remember grace. Once, we were wretched sinners, far from Christ and His ways. We were headed toward destruction. But grace came to us, sought us, bought us, rescued us, and washed us. And just in case we missed Paul's earlier point, he spelled it out: "He saved us, not on the basis of deeds which we have done in righteousness, but according to his mercy" (Titus 3:5, paraphrase). We didn't earn merit badges to get salvation. By pointing out the grace that has brought us here and how far we've come, Paul hoped to stir us up to give more grace to others. In Titus 3:1, he wrote, "Be ready for every good work."

The grace of God's cleansing work should lead us to be ready for every good work. Because we are parents of toddlers, remembering we've been washed in grace is especially important. As our toddlers try our patience, push us to our limits, fuss, and show selfish behavior, we can remember the grace we've received and, by the Spirit's help, offer the grace they need.

What is bath time like for your little one? Does your toddler love the water or hate it? What have been your favorite moments so far when it comes to tub time? If it's been an ordeal, what would your toddler rather be doing?

_____

_____

_____

_____

_____

_____

When and how did God bring you to salvation? How does the grace He showed you then motivate you today?

_____

_____

_____

_____

_____

_____

The Washing of Baptism

"Why are you waiting? Arise and be baptized, and wash away your sins."
ACTS 22:16

As we continue to think on the theme of cleansing in the Bible, let's dig into Acts 22. Here, Paul described his conversion and subsequent baptism. In his testimony, Paul recalled asking God, "What shall I do, Lord?" (v. 10). God told him to go Damascus, where a man named Ananias said, "Why are you waiting? Arise and be baptized." While Christians may disagree on the timing and methods of baptism, most can agree that baptism is always a fitting response to what God has done for the convert, a sign and seal of regeneration and the remission of sins.

Just as the dove hovered over Jesus at His baptism, we are reminded of the Spirit of God hovering over the waters in creation (Luke 3:22; Genesis 1:2), reminding us that God is remaking us. Baptism whispers the memory of the flood of God's judgment against sin, judgment that our sins deserve. And baptism reminds us of how God brought the Israelites through the Red Sea, liberating them to freedom, just as He has liberated us from the bondage of sin.

Are you baptized? If not, consider Ananias's question: "Why are you waiting?" If you are already baptized, thank God for the rich meaning of your baptism. Thank Him for sending His Holy Spirit into your life, for bringing you through the flood of judgment you deserved, for rescuing you from the slavery of sin, and for drawing you close through cleansing. Praise God for washing away your sins! If you haven't explored the subject of baptism or thought about it since having children, now is a good time to dig deeper in God's Word and know your beliefs.

Cleansing Begins
with Obedience

Elisha sent a messenger to him, saying, "Go and
wash in the Jordan seven times, and your flesh
shall be restored to you, and you shall be clean."
2 KINGS 5:10

A s moms, sometimes we have the tendency to overcomplicate things. Maybe you leave directions for the babysitter: "At bedtime, make sure that Avery has her footed pj's, nighttime diaper, stuffed animal, and sippy cup of water. Read three board books, say prayers, and tuck her in. Close the door, but leave the hall light on and the night-light in the bathroom."

In the story of Naaman, the leper who sought the prophet Elisha's help for healing, we find someone else who wanted to overcomplicate things. When Elisha sent word that the way to be healed was simple— wash seven times in the Jordan—Naaman thought surely it had to be more involved than that. Surely the prophet would come out to him and wave his hands over him or perhaps send him to one of the rivers of Damascus (they were cleaner rivers after all). But really, all God wanted from Naaman was faith and humble obedience. God would cleanse if Naaman would obey.

Sometimes we are this way with God too. We want Him to do some great work in our lives (heal our marriage, help our crushing debt, banish our anxiety), and we're willing to go to such great lengths to have Him heal us, yet we're not willing to do the smallest work of humbling ourselves in obedience. God longs to cleanse us. But healing waters can't heal those who won't get into them.

Running to God

Draw near to God and He will draw near to you. Cleanse your hands, you sinners; and purify your hearts, you double-minded.
JAMES 4:8

Have you found your toddler hiding in the laundry room with a nabbed cookie yet or hiding under a blanket with marker smeared all over his face? It's human nature to hide when we've done wrong. We want to run out of the light, into the shadows. Adam and Eve did. You have. And your toddler will at some point.

But God wants us to do the counterintuitive thing. When we sin, He wants us to draw near to Him. He promises that as we draw near to Him, He will draw near to us. But we can't draw near unchanged. We must be cleansed. We must repent. This is not the ceremonial—the outward-only—cleansing that the Pharisees chided the disciples for not observing (Matthew 15:1–20). No, God looks on the heart. He wants the clean hands of a pure heart, of one who has renounced the false idols that woo us away from Him (Psalm 24:4). He reminds us we cannot be double-minded as we come to Him, trying to keep one foot in the world's ways and one in God's. No, "If the LORD is God, follow Him" (1 Kings 18:21). There is no room for wavering.

When you sin, run to Jesus in repentance. Renounce your desire to live a double life. And ask God to cleanse you from the inside out and strengthen you to choose right.

What mischief or mayhem has your toddler created lately? Have you been able to laugh about it yet?

_____

_____

_____

_____

_____

_____

_____

_____

_____

_____

Write a note to your little one here about when you became a Christian or were baptized.

_____

_____

_____

_____

_____

_____

_____

_____

The Anatomy of Confession

*Wash me thoroughly from my iniquity,
and cleanse me from my sin.*
PSALM 51:2

Your little one's vocabulary is growing by the day whether or not their spoken words are. Bath time can be a fun time to work on words for body parts. "Now we're going to wash your toes. Show me your toes!" Giggles ensue as you soap up those little piggies. Just as it's good to give your child the vocabulary for their anatomy, God has given us an understanding of the anatomy of a good confession through David's own recorded prayer in Psalm 51. He wrote this psalm after he committed adultery with Bathsheba and had her husband, Uriah, sent to the front lines of battle, where he was killed.

The prayer for cleansing begins with a cry for mercy and a declaration that our God is a God of steadfast love (or *hesed*, in Hebrew: covenant faithfulness) and abundant mercy. And then there is the plea, "Blot out my transgressions. Wash me thoroughly from my iniquity, and cleanse me from my sin" (Psalm 51:1–2). David realized he could not wash himself. He needed God to do it. So he ran toward God, not away, and asked! Also, he understood that there were many sins involved in this transgression, not just the obvious ones of adultery and murder. There were countless distortions of the truth along the way.

But David acknowledged that his betrayal was not just against Uriah but against God. This is where turning from sin and growing in grace begins: believing in God's mercy and asking for it, acknowledging sin and requesting cleansing. We'd do well to study this anatomy of a confession.

The Anatomy of Confession, Part II

Purge me with hyssop, and I shall be clean;
wash me, and I shall be whiter than snow.
PSALM 51:7

Repentance and faith: it's funny how the first two steps of the gospel life are the steps we continue to take each day of the journey. It is the basic method for growth. That doesn't mean we need to continue confessing old sins. No, He is faithful and just to forgive us of those sins. But it does mean that with each new day, new sin invades our hearts and minds, and we must be quick to do again what we did at the beginning, to draw near to God in repentance and faith.

As we continue to look at how Psalm 51 shows us the anatomy of a good confession, I love the simple faith of David we see in these verses. He'd committed a sin so grievous that if we did it today and were caught, we'd probably go to prison for life. Yet David said with finality, "Purge me with hyssop, and I shall be clean." David had faith that no matter how great the sin, God could cleanse him of it completely. And he'd be not just cleaner but truly, objectively, 100 percent clean.

Parenting is humbling. Our patience is tried daily. Our inherent self-ishness collides with daily requirements for service. We must choose day in and day out between self-centered living and others-centered living as toddlers demand our attention, our time, and our resources. Parenting can be a major part of God's sanctification for us if we will use these moments that reveal our sinful tendencies to run to God and not away. Like David, we can be confident in God's cleansing power.

The Anatomy of Confession, Part III

Create in me a clean heart, O God, and renew a steadfast spirit within me.
PSALM 51:10

So far, as we've looked at the anatomy of a true confession, we've seen admitting wrong, taking responsibility, asking forgiveness, and believing in God's ability to restore and cleanse. At this point in David's prayer, he turned his focus inward, asking God to create in him a clean heart and to renew him for a future steadfast life of service. The point of repentance is not just to bring us into neutral territory again but to restore and renew us to worship and service.

Here David envisioned a future life of faith and good works: "Then I will teach transgressors Your ways, and sinners shall be converted to You" (Psalm 51:13). He also envisioned raising his voice in praise: "And my tongue shall sing aloud of Your righteousness. O Lord, open my lips" (vv. 14–15). God doesn't want us to continue lurking in hiding after we've sinned. He wants us back! He wants us to come, confess, repent, believe, receive, and be restored. He wants our fruitful service once more.

In marriage and in parenting, our sinful tendencies can sideline us. We lash out at a spouse in anger, and rather than repent, we silently sulk or withdraw. Or with our toddlers, we find ourselves wanting to cocoon in comfort and tune out. Sin would keep us on the bench, but true repentance spurs us onto the field, into the active zone. It leads us to work toward creating joy in our marriages, to engage our toddlers with attention and love, correction and instruction. And as we experience grace, it helps us raise our own voices in praise. The repentant woman finds herself praising God for His compassion. She longs to extend that compassion. Though she often fails, true repentance leads her toward the active work of creating harmony in her home and lending her grateful voice in praise. Create in us a clean heart, O Lord, that we might lead others to You!

Our little ones give us eyes to see the world around us with new wonder. I loved watching my little guy delight and giggle at how the waves kept coming back to tickle his feet or seeing my firstborn with nose pressed to the glass watching the falling snow. What wonders is your toddler helping you to see anew these days?

_____

_____

_____

Psalm 51 also talks about restoring the joy of our salvation. Write a prayer asking God to renew and restore to you the joy you had when you first believed.

_____

_____

_____

_____

An Ongoing Need

*Who gave Himself for us, that He might
redeem us from every lawless deed
and purify for Himself His own special
people, zealous for good works.*
TITUS 2:14

Why did Christ give Himself for us? Here in this passage from Titus, Paul said that the purpose was to redeem and purify for Himself a people of His own, zealous for good works. Here are a few important things for us to know about sanctification: Without Christ, this work would be useless. We are "sanctified by the Holy Spirit," and it is "by the Spirit" that we are able to "put to death the deeds of the body" (Romans 15:16; 8:13).

But unlike justification, which is entirely God's work, our sanctification requires our cooperation. Listen to the imperatives in Galatians 5: "walk by the Spirit" (v. 16 NIV), "live by the Spirit" (v. 25 NIV), and "keep in step with the Spirit" (v. 25 NIV). God holds us accountable for our participation. And, unlike justification, which is finished, sanctification is ongoing. The Greek verb *peripateo*, translated "walk by the spirit," literally means "to go about" or "to walk around." Paul deliberately used a verb tense to communicate unceasing, ongoing activity.

As your toddler has learned or is learning to walk, it has been with unceasing, ongoing practice. As your toddler reminds you each day, the need for cleansing is ongoing, unceasing. These little touch points can be reminders for us, too, that our need for sanctification is ongoing and demands our participation.

Purify Your Hearts

*"Hear and understand: Not what goes into
the mouth defiles a man; but what comes
out of the mouth, this defiles a man."*
MATTHEW 15:10–11

When it comes to our sanctification, God is much more interested in what is going on inside us than in appearances. The Pharisees were obsessed with outward conformity, but time and again Jesus asked them to examine their hearts. Here is no exception. They had confronted Jesus about His disciples' failure to wash their hands. In turn, Jesus explained that it is not what goes into a man that defiles him but what comes out—his sinful words and actions that come from a sinful heart. He returned to the prophets and quoted the words of Isaiah: "These people draw near to Me with their mouth, and honor Me with their lips, but their heart is far from Me" (Matthew 15:8).

It's easy for us to wag our heads at the Pharisees here and miss the point. Jesus wants us to examine our own hearts. He gives us a good test in Luke 6:45: "Out of the abundance of the heart [the] mouth speaks." Listen to the words of your mouth when your toddler makes a mess for the umpteenth time or when the driver in front of you is driving too slowly and you are crunched for time. What words come out of your mouth when you see your next-door neighbor returning from the vacation you can only dream about or when the promotion your spouse was hoping for goes to another? Demeaning words, demanding words, discontent words, critical words, cynical words—these are clues to the state of our hearts. Jesus didn't mince words with the Pharisees on this, and He loves us enough to convict us of it also. Ask God to cleanse not just the outside of you but the inside.

Washing of Sanctification

Husbands, love your wives, just as Christ also loved the church and gave Himself for her, that He might sanctify and cleanse her with the washing of water by the word.
EPHESIANS 5:25–26

If you are married, you and your spouse have the chance to be a living picture for your toddler of Jesus and His love. In a sense, your marriage is their first picture book of Christ's love for the church. As a husband loves his wife and lays his life down for her, as a wife honors and submits to her husband in the context of love, our children see what Paul called "a great mystery" (Ephesians 5:32): Christ's love for His bride, the church. But here in this famous passage on marriage, not only does God give us insight into how to love well but also into how sanctification happens: through the cleansing power of the Word.

This echoes Christ's own words in the Gospel of John when He prayed for us. He cried to the Father, "Sanctify them by Your truth. Your word is truth" (John 17:17). Paul knew that the Scriptures train us in righteousness so that we may be "thoroughly equipped" (2 Timothy 3:17). How then does the Word cleanse us? What exactly does it do? As Paul wrote, "All Scripture is given by inspiration of God, and is profitable for doctrine, for reproof, for correction, [and] for instruction in righteousness" (v. 16). For us, then, as we read the Word, pray over it, and allow it to convict us and draw us to Christ, we are doing what God has called us to do: make ready for His return. We are washing ourselves, scrubbing out the spots, ironing the wrinkles, that we might be a radiant church—a beautiful bride—ready for that day when we will be presented to Christ, our Bridegroom.

What little victories has your toddler had lately? Has she mastered a new skill or gotten more fluid with an old one?

_____

_____

_____

_____

_____

_____

How do you find the Word of God changing you most often? Bringing conviction, encouragement, joy, instruction, or a sense of fullness? Maybe it's a little of all of these. Thank God for giving us His Word that our ongoing journey in sanctification might continue.

_____

_____

_____

_____

_____

_____

_____

FIVE
Abiding

Your Sixteen-Month-Old,

Developmental Guide

Was that a streak of lightning or your toddler that just flashed by? He is likely on the move this month. If he has mastered walking, new skills are not far behind: running, dancing, and climbing! Watch out, world—here he comes!

You may have to up your babyproofing game and think like a toddler, particularly if you have a climber. Make sure furniture is attached to walls and sharp and dangerous objects are put out of reach or locked when not in use. Or if your little one is not yet walking by sixteen months (like my firstborn), it is still in a developmentally appropriate range, but you may want to talk to your pediatrician, who can give you an idea of strategies to try and when to seek help.

It's likely your toddler may be exploring her full emotional range these days. One minute she is happily playing. The next she is a pool of tears. A while later, she is giggling and hugging you, only to be angry or solitary the next moment. Not to worry, this is standard toddler behavior.

But you have an important role to play as she learns how to handle these wild emotions that sweep her up from one minute to the next. You can help her know those emotions are normal. You model that you can remain calm through distressing emotions, but also that you can be an empathetic responder: "Oh, I see how sad you are that your tower fell. Can I give you a hug? Now, can I help you rebuild it?" Your responses are teaching her how to regulate emotions and how to respond to setbacks. And God is giving you many teachable moments these days!

Just as your toddler may be testing out his emotional range, he is probably also testing out his vocal range. From experimenting with sounds (and volumes!) to trying out new words and ways of communicating, your little one is actively expanding his ability to communicate. Don't worry if his vocabulary is still very limited. On average, toddlers have about ten to fifteen words mastered by sixteen to eighteen months. That means your little guy may have more words or fewer and still be right on track.

But you can play a huge role in the expansion of those skills. Hopefully, you are already increasing them daily by reading lots of books and by narrating everyday things you are doing. This narration may feel awkward at first, but it greatly helps your little one to learn about her world and grow in her ability to communicate. Narrating is simply saying aloud the things you are doing: "We are walking down the stairs, aren't we?" or "Now I carry my plate to the kitchen."

This is an exciting time of exploration for your toddler. And you are giving your little one the love and the tools he needs to grow in his mastery of the world.

Developmental Focus: Attachment

Attachment is one of those parenting buzzwords that is thrown around so much that we may have heard it but not truly know what it means. Or we may have heard of it in connection with one particular type of parenting strategy that is not our own and dismissed it because we don't follow that particular strategy. Attachment isn't a philosophy of parenting so much as it is a goal for every loving parent. To put it simply, attachment in psychological terms is the relationship between a child and his caregiver that results in him feeling secure, safe, and protected. Attachment stabilizes the child in the world.

Attachment isn't the same as bonding, though some mistakenly use these terms synonymously. Beginning around six months, an infant can start to anticipate the response of the caregiver. Psychologists classify it in one of four ways: sensitive (in a loving way), insensitive (in a rejecting way), insensitive (in an inconsistent way), or atypical (in a disorganized way).[3] The child who receives the sensitive, loving care develops a secure attachment, while children whose caregivers respond in other ways become children who avoid or withdraw from the caregiver. A secure attachment is vital to your toddler's ability to flourish in a number of ways. But perhaps most importantly, it plays a significant role in brain development. A secure attachment enables the brain to focus on higher levels of learning. And it enables the child to move with confidence and security into the risks involved in learning, knowing that there is a responsive, loving parent available when she meets with distress or frustration.

This Month's Spiritual Focus: Abiding

We've been looking at all the ways we, like children, grow in grace: from walking with Christ to imitating Him, resting in Him, and being washed by His Spirit. This month our spiritual focus is on abiding with Christ, that is, dwelling with Him or making our home in Him. One of the central metaphors for abiding is attachment to the Vine, and we'll be looking in detail at how this metaphor informs our faith.

Abiding Is No Great Mystery

*"Behold, I stand at the door and knock. If anyone
hears My voice and opens the door, I will come
in to him and dine with him, and he with Me."*
REVELATION 3:20

This month we'll focus on what it means to abide in or hold fast to Christ. This frequent command in the New Testament has often been misunderstood to be some vague, mystical experience. In reality, abiding in Christ is evidence of our salvation. It denotes not just a superficial acquaintance but an intimate relationship with Jesus. In Revelation, John compares this union to a fellowship meal. The Greek word for abide also means to make our home with or dwell with someone. To abide with Christ is an ongoing, intimate communion, as if we shared our home and table with Him on an ongoing basis.

Our toddlers share life with us like this in a physical sense. As we care for their needs day by day, they come to know us as a place of security. We become a safe haven for them, and this gives them the confidence to venture out into the world. In child psychology terms, we call this a securely attached child. In biblical terms, we might call this a child who has consistently abided in the love of a parent or caregiver. Either way, we know that this kind of nurturing and communion produces the fruit of confidence.

In our spiritual lives, abiding with Christ should also produce a confidence. We know we are loved and secure in the Father. We know we have a refuge. That should give us the confidence to venture out in faith and good works.

Abiding Is Mutual Connection

Your Sixteen-Month-Old, Week One

"Abide in Me, and I in you."
JOHN 15:4 ESV

There is a beautiful mutuality to the command "Abide in Me." Within this command hides the wonder of our union with Christ. You abide in Him, and He abides in you. Notice how a branch is connected to the vine and the vine to the branch; there is a mutual connection. Isn't it a marvel that God condescends to connect with us?

Fellowship is at the heart. He makes His home with us and we with Him. We share life. We share joy. This is the fulfillment of so many Old Testament images. Remember how God appeared to the Israelites shortly after they left Egypt? A pillar of cloud by day and fire by night to lead them—God showed His heart to be *with* His people, to guide them and abide with them (Exodus 13:21–22). By the time of the kings, again, we see God's heart to be among His people as He allowed Solomon to fulfill David's prayer to build a permanent "house" for God among His people (1 Chronicles 28). Fast-forward to Jesus, our Immanuel, our God *with us* . . . Are you starting to see a pattern? God wants to be *with* His people.

For our toddlers, the sunshine of our enjoyment of them gives them their first taste of what it is to be truly loved and delighted in. You may not realize it, but every time you exchange smiles, hugs, and looks of understanding, you are giving them the mutual connection that will matter for every other relationship they will know in life.

Abiding Is Dependence

As the branch cannot bear fruit by itself, unless it abides in the vine, neither can you, unless you abide in me. I am the vine; you are the branches. Whoever abides in me and I in him, he it is that bears much fruit, for apart from me you can do nothing.
JOHN 15:4–5 ESV

These days your toddler still depends on you for everything. He is dependent on your provision of food, your changing of his diaper, and your caring for his needs. Without you, your toddler would be lost. While this dependence won't go on forever, for now this constant care for his needs can be a catalyst to remember your own dependence on Christ.

Dependence is an important aspect of abiding in Christ. Unlike the mutuality of connection, dependence is one-way. The branch depends upon the vine and derives its vitality from the vine. Without the vine, it is utterly impotent. Indeed, without the vine, it is dead. With the vital life-flowing sustenance of the vine, the branch can blossom and slowly ripen, creating fruit.

This is not a new theme in the Scriptures. Notice the similarity to the tree that flourishes beside the stream (Psalm 1:3). Or the metaphor in the book of Colossians of the head and the body: without the head we are powerless (1:18). Meanwhile, the writer of Hebrews continued the lesson of dependence with Christ as the author and finisher of our faith (12:2). Again and again, God brings home to us our utter need of Him and the amazing power that flows through us as a result of our connection.

While our toddlers can and should outgrow their utter dependence on us, we will never outgrow our dependence on Christ. This dependence is not a liability but the source of our power.

Does your little one still like to be held and cuddled, or are you noticing a burgeoning independence these days, or perhaps a mixture of both?

_____

_____

_____

_____

_____

_____

_____

What does it mean to you to know that God desires to be _with_ you? How does this change how you think about your union or abiding with Christ?

_____

_____

_____

_____

_____

_____

_____

_____

Abiding in His Word

So Jesus said to the Jews who had believed him, "If you abide in my word, you are truly my disciples, and you will know the truth, and the truth will set you free."
JOHN 8:31–32 ESV

What does it mean to abide in Christ? Is it mystical, or are there ordinary, concrete steps we can take to abide with Him? Jesus told a crowd that to abide in His Word is to truly be His disciple. But I love how simply He brought it home to us in the story of Martha and Mary. You remember how busy Martha was preparing a meal for their visitors. I think it is so easy for busy moms to identify with Martha. She was the one paying attention to the details of all these hungry men in her home—who inevitably were going to want to be fed—am I right? Meanwhile, Mary took the posture of pupil—sitting at the feet of Rabbi Jesus, listening, learning, drawing close.

Jesus lovingly chided Martha, "My dear Martha, you are worried and upset over all these details! There is only one thing worth being concerned about. Mary has discovered it, and it will not be taken away from her" (Luke 10:41–42 NLT). I feel so often like Martha: distracted. It sure would be nice to have Jesus turn my head toward Him and say, "Here's the one thing I want you to focus on." And that's what He does. For Mary and Martha it meant literally sitting at Jesus' feet. For us, it is sitting before His Word, reading it, meditating on it, and memorizing it. I know how hard it is to make time for this in the busy days of running after a toddler, but let me encourage you to not neglect it. Our souls need it.

Abiding Is Keeping His Commands

"If you keep My commandments, you will abide in My love, just as I have kept My Father's commandments and abide in His love."
JOHN 15:10

Undoubtedly, you have spent some time babyproofing your home: locking away dangerous cleaning fluids, putting sharp objects high out of reach, making sure that gates are in place on your stairs to keep your little one from falling. In the areas where your toddler can go, you have made sure to have toys and all kinds of pleasant things for him to enjoy. But maybe your little one, like mine, will sometimes stand at the edge of a baby gate and whine.

Why have you put boundaries in place in your home? Is it to deny your child pleasure, or is it to protect him? Likewise, God's commandments— His boundary lines in our lives—are perfect. They aren't rules meant to confine and constrain us. They are commands of perfect wisdom designed to give us the most abundant and joyful life possible. They don't guarantee our health and wealth. But they do represent life and fullness and freedom.

To keep these commands is to abide in His love—it is to stay within the pleasant pastures He has outlined for us. It is to agree with the psalmist that "the boundary lines have fallen for me in pleasant places; surely I have a delightful inheritance" (Psalm 16:6 NIV). Keeping His commands is staying within the fence He has lovingly built for us. It is staying in the pleasant places, the verdant pastures. We abide in Him and His love by keeping these commands.

Abiding Changes Our Minds

*If then you were raised with Christ, seek those
things which are above, where Christ is, sitting
at the right hand of God. Set your mind on
things above, not on things on the earth.*
COLOSSIANS 3:1–2

D id you know that on average it takes a toddler up to twenty exposures to a new food to become acclimated to it? Little by little, with enough repeat exposure, they find their tastes changing. Perhaps you have at some point changed a habit and found your tastes changing with it. Maybe you have opted for healthier foods and then found your cravings actually changing from donuts to a crisp ripe apple or a slice of avocado. Change is funny that way. If we are diligent about being in God's Word and filling our minds with it, we will notice as it begins to transform our wills and our affections.

Consider the words of James: "You ask and do not receive, because you ask amiss, that you may spend it on your pleasures" (James 4:3). We see here someone whose mind and therefore affections have not been changed or shaped by the Word. As we dwell on God's Word, as His Spirit fills us, we begin to crave good things, spiritually healthy things. We find these words of John becoming true in our lives: "You will ask what you desire, and it shall be done for you" (John 15:7). This promise that is so often misappropriated makes sense, however, when you think of a person whose mind and therefore desires are changing to align with God's heart and will. As we set our minds on things above, our desires for His will on the earth below will characterize our longings and prayers.

There are lots of frustrating moments for toddlers. As our children grow, it's important for us as parents to praise their efforts and not just the results. Where have you been noticing your child's efforts as he or she works at acquiring new skills?

_____

_____

_____

_____

_____

_____

We read David's words in Psalm 16:6 that the boundary lines have fallen for him in pleasant places. How do you see God's commands making your life sweeter than it would be if you disregarded those commands?

_____

_____

_____

_____

_____

_____

Abiding in His Love

Abide in My love.
JOHN 15:9

Did you know that being well loved and bonded to a parent actually strengthens a toddler's brain? Your toddler's brain is growing at an unprecedented rate during the first three years of her life. And your little one's experiences affect how the brain grows. The ready availability of love, affection, and security frees the brain to focus on mastering more complex tasks. Studies of neglected children in Romanian orphanages have given insight into the long-term repercussions of the lack of secure attachment in early childhood. (While God in His grace can certainly heal these wounds if you have adopted a son or daughter with a similar story, it underlines just how precious your attachment with your son or daughter will be as God works to heal these painful parts.)

While our brains and bodies as adults are not growing at the same rate as those of our toddlers, it is little wonder that our security in Christ, our sense of being in His love, has wide-ranging repercussions. It affects our mental health, our self-confidence, even our ability to take risks or not place excessive value on the opinions of others. When we follow the command to abide in His love, we rest in the love of Christ. We rest in the love of the One who laid down His life for us. As we consider daily the cross of Christ, we can have undeniable confidence, and we can move in the world with the assurance that no matter what comes our way, we are loved by God. As we abide in that love, we abide in His power, strength, and joy. Abide in His love, and it will abound in far-reaching ways.

Abiding Means Being Fruitful

I am the vine; you are the branches. Whoever abides in me and I in him, he it is that bears much fruit, for apart from me you can do nothing.
JOHN 15:5 ESV

I love how God builds the themes of death and resurrection into the fabric of creation itself. From the falling leaves to the budding flowers of spring, from the decomposing soil that makes new plants grow to the caterpillar and its chrysalis, we see these themes everywhere and can point them out to our children as they grow. One of my favorite places to notice death and resurrection is in the apple tree. I love to show my children an apple's secret. If we pluck an apple and cut it in half across its equator, so to speak, we can see its story. Inside is what looks like a star or the flower that came before the fruit. Remember the beautiful apple blossoms that covered the trees a few short months ago? The death of the blossoms coincided with the birth of the fruit.

We hear the echo of Christ's words in this: "Unless a grain of wheat falls into the ground and dies, it remains alone; but if it dies, it produces much grain. He who loves his life will lose it, and he who hates his life in this world will keep it for eternal life" (John 12:24–25). As we die to ourselves, as our blossoms fade, something even greater begins to happen. Imperceptibly something is born. It ripens over time. And the beauty of this new thing is more than just a wonder for the eyes—it is a nourishing, life-giving fruit. Perhaps motherhood has required a special kind of dying to self for you. But here's the beauty in those places where you have died to self: those are the very places God is bringing to life the miracle of something even more beautiful and nourishing.

95

Abiding Means Accepting Pruning

"Every branch in Me that does not bear fruit
He takes away; and every branch that bears
fruit He prunes, that it may bear more fruit."
JOHN 15:2

Every so often as a parent we have to make our toddler more uncomfortable in order to make him feel better. We're the ones that have to pull the splinter from the wriggling finger, apply antiseptic to a scraped knee, or help them through routine vaccinations. Our love for them is so great that we would not let an ounce of pain come their way unless it was absolutely necessary for a greater gain in their life.

Likewise, abiding in Christ sometimes means submitting to the pruning hand of the Master Gardener, our good and faithful God. Our omniscient God knows exactly when to trim and what not to touch to make His vine as fruitful as possible. His pruning isn't haphazard. It isn't maniacal. It is careful, purposeful, and perfect for the health of the fruit He is cultivating. We can trust the Master Gardener; He will not allow one iota of pain more than is necessary for our fruitfulness. And He will not waste one ounce of that pain but will use it all to transform us and bring glory to His name in ways that we cannot yet ask or imagine. Notice that while we are being pruned, we are also being sustained internally by the flow of the life of Christ in our connection to the vine. Inside and outside, we are being sustained and cultivated. The union of Christ is nourishing us, while God's painful Providence prunes us—all that we might be abundantly fruitful.

The love you are pouring into your child now will affect future generations. Imagine that! In what ways are you bonding and showing affection to your toddler? How is your little one expressing his or her affection for you?

_____

_____

_____

_____

_____

_____

Where do you see mature fruit in your own life, or where do you see evidence of fruit in the first stages of ripening?

_____

_____

_____

_____

_____

_____

Abiding Means to Persevere

*"If you abide in My word, you
are My disciples indeed."*
JOHN 8:31

Often in the parables we see that it may be difficult to distinguish between the saved and the unsaved. The wheat and the tares grow side by side (Matthew 13:24–30). The sheep and the goats are intermingled (25:31–46). Even Judas was mixed in with the eleven other disciples but wasn't truly one of them (John 13:10–11). These passages do *not* indicate that we can lose our salvation but rather that one of the true tests of our salvation is our perseverance in faith.

The Bible is adamant that our salvation begins and ends with grace (Galatians 3:2–3) and that no one can snatch us out of the Good Shepherd's hand (John 10:27–30). Those branches that are cut off and cast away from the True Vine (15:6) are the branches that were never truly connected (saved) to begin with: the pretenders. Their departure is a sign that they were not truly His (1 John 2:19). For us, we can take comfort in the fact "that He who has begun a good work in you will complete it" (Philippians 1:6) while also finding motivation that if we are far from Jesus, we need to return and repent. Both Peter and Judas denied Christ, but only one repented and returned.

This should give us pause if we have sin in our lives that we just aren't willing to give up. Moms, you may be busier than you've ever been in these days of balancing the needs of a toddler and other responsibilities, but don't neglect repentance. Take time to examine your heart and see if you are clinging more closely to some sinful pattern than to Him. If so, don't delay—run to Jesus.

Abiding More and More

"These things I have spoken to you,
that My joy may remain in you,
and that your joy may be full"
JOHN 15:11

We've been looking in-depth over these past weeks at the parable of the True Vine. This parable does not indicate that some Christians abide and some do not. As we saw yesterday, there are some who are not truly His but are only pretenders. These are cut off (John 15:6). All those who are truly saved are attached to the Vine. But the Bible does indicate that there are degrees by which we can experience the reality of this connection more and more.

For instance, you can become more joyful. Jesus said these things not only because He wants us to have joy but because He wants us to have full joy. We can enjoy Jesus more deeply. We can bear more fruit. The passage not only indicates we can bear fruit but that we can bear "more fruit" (v. 2) and "much fruit" (v. 8). And we can grow in our likeness to Christ by degrees (see 2 Corinthians 3:18, for instance).

Let us then press on to grow in our abiding faith in Jesus. How can you saturate yourself in His Word despite the busy season of mothering that you're in? Could you listen to the Word on audio while you do household chores, put on worship music and sing and dance with your toddler, or take a verse with you on an index card to memorize or meditate upon as you push your toddler in the stroller? Let us pour over His Word more and have our minds and affections transformed. Let our fruit abound and with it our joy. Let us abide more and more.

Abiding for His Glory

"By this my Father is glorified, that you bear much fruit and so prove to be my disciples."
JOHN 15:8 ESV

As we wrap up this month's focus on abiding, we remember that our abiding has a goal—a purpose. Our connection to the Vine produces fruit, and that fruit's purpose is to bring glory to the Father. The fruit doesn't exist to receive its own praise. Its purpose is to testify to the goodness of the Gardener, His faithful care of His branches, and His skills in planting, pruning, and husbanding. The Father, the Vinedresser, rightly receives the glory for the harvest because His role is not passive but an active, initiating, sustaining, and nurturing one.

This should encourage us in two ways. First, our God is active in our lives. We do not believe, like the deists, in a distant God who wound the clock of creation and then stepped away, letting everything tick on. We believe in an up-close, personal God who tends to us like the most careful of gardeners, diligent to allow nothing into His prized vineyard but that which will nurture the vines. We can trust that if we feel the shears, it is because He knows absolutely it is what we need. And it should encourage us that we exist *on purpose*. We are designed for a reason: to bring glory to God by bearing fruit. You are no accident. You are a purposeful part of bringing joy to the Vinedresser's heart. And one of your purposes—one of your callings in which you are to bear fruit—is as a mother. Every day as you care for your little one's physical and emotional needs, as you treat him or her as a precious soul entrusted to your care, you are living out your purpose to the glory of God.

Your toddler is growing day by day. What words or new ways to communicate has he or she found lately?

_____

_____

_____

_____

_____

_____

_____

Write a prayer below that you may abide more and more in Christ—that your fruit may abound, that your joy may be full, that your likeness may be more and more like Christ. Ask that God would do this for His glory.

_____

_____

_____

_____

_____

_____

_____

SIX

Feeding

Your Seventeen-Month-Old, Developmental Guide

It's a good thing your toddler is on the go these days because he or she is probably starting to get heavy. According to the World Health Organization, the median weight of a seventeen-month-old is 22.1 pounds for girls and 23.7 pounds for boys. The median height is 31.4 inches for girls and 32.0 inches for boys. No wonder mamas are strong; that's a couple sacks of potatoes' worth of toddler to lift.

Some parents may be wondering if their little ones will add any pounds this month. Between picky eating, teething, and the go-go-go that characterizes kids of this age, sometimes getting the nutrition into them is tough. Give your little one the opportunity to eat three meals and three snacks spaced regularly throughout the day, as well as three to four cups of milk. That way even if he rejects food at one opportunity, he'll get it at the next.

Your little one is probably getting a bit more coordinated, especially with her hands. As she develops that pincer grasp, she may be picking up crayons and scribbling. Or she may be moving objects from one place to another and stacking blocks or cups. Encourage her with modeling clay or playdough. The squeezing, rolling, and shaping will build hand strength and dexterity.

She may even have the dexterity to brush her own teeth (with help, of course, until she's much older). But the practice of moving the toothbrush and controlling her hands will not only help her grow her skills but quite possibly make toothbrushing less of a chore. Remember to use a pea-sized amount of toothpaste and to make sure you are going over what she's done when she's finished or guiding her hand along the way.

Your little one may be down to just one nap now, albeit a longer one—hopefully about two hours in the afternoon. Remember that these naps are important for your child, and try to help him keep the habit of napping for a while. If you are wondering, typically only 2.5 percent of children will give up napping by their second birthday, while 94 percent of children will give up napping by age five. When your child does begin transitioning away from naps, it's helpful to still keep a quiet rest time in the afternoons. It gives you both a bit of a respite and may help your child learn to enjoy independent play or, later, reading.

Developmental Focus: Feeding

Toddlers are notoriously picky eaters. This is the age where you may despair if they will ever get past it and eat a healthy, well-balanced meal. Here are a few things to keep in mind:

- *Don't stop offering.* Your little one may show dislike for a certain food one night and love it the next time it is offered. Just because he doesn't like something at one meal doesn't necessarily mean he won't enjoy it at the next. Don't write off foods as dislikes prematurely, particularly healthy foods.

- *Don't force food.* As the expression goes, you can lead a horse to water, but you can't make it drink. The same holds true for the toddler with a mind of his own. Don't force foods. Be creative, try the airplane bit—zooming it into his mouth—but don't press if there's resistance. There's always next time.
- *Let your child help.* Sometimes letting your little one break lettuce leaves for the salad or put small bits of chopped tomato in the bowl will make him more ready to give those same foods a try.
- *Keep mealtimes focused.* Sit down to a meal together as a family at the table without distractions of TV or electronics. Help mealtimes be relaxed, not rushed, and focused on connecting with one another. A peaceful, calm atmosphere will go a long way. Also, if you are making a dish that is extra spicy, pull out a little portion of the food for your toddler before adding the intense spice.
- *Keep seated.* A high chair is often still very helpful at this point to make sure your toddler stays seated during mealtimes. Not only is this important to prevent choking, but it also means it's more likely he'll actually eat something.
- *Small bites.* Continue to make sure your toddler's food is cut small enough and not served too hot. Help keep your toddler from choking or getting burned.

This Month's Spiritual Focus:
Spiritual Nourishment

Just as your toddler needs the right physical nourishment, you need the right spiritual nourishment as you grow as a child of God. The Bible frequently employs metaphors of feeding and feasting on Christ. This month we'll explore those images and what they reveal about God's commands, the person of Jesus, and our future hope.

Savoring His Statutes

More to be desired are they than gold,
yea, than much fine gold; sweeter also
than honey and the honeycomb.
PSALM 19:10

Chances are that when your little one first started solid foods, you could see a natural preference for the sweeter ones: the pureed sweet potatoes, the pears, and the applesauce. From infancy, we understand that sweetness is pleasing. And when it comes to the Word of God, the psalmist found words to describe it in comparison to the sweetest thing he knew: honey from the honeycomb.

In the verses preceding, David recounted the perfections of the law of God. He savored them bite by bite, like someone lingering over a rich slice of chocolate cake. He described God's law as "perfect" and able to convert the soul (Psalm 19:7). We will not find God's Word lacking: it is sufficient for all our needs (2 Timothy 3:16–17). And it is living—having the power to actually change us from the inside out (Hebrews 4:12). David praised it for being "sure" or dependable and for "making wise the simple" (Psalm 19:7). He went on to describe God's statutes as "right," "pure," "clean," "true," and "righteous." He told us that they "rejoice the heart," "enlighten the eyes," and "endure forever" (vv. 7–9). Why take time to praise God's Word? When we savor all the ways God's Word is for us, we remember how God is for us. How He provides all our needs, gives us what is best, and brings delight to our lives!

The Sweetest Thing

My son, eat honey, for it is good, yes, the honey from the comb is sweet to your taste; know that wisdom is the same for your soul; if you find it, then there will be a future, and your hope will not be cut off.

PROVERBS 24:13–14 NASB 1995

The American Academy of Pediatrics advises that children under two should avoid added sugars in their diet. But with sugars hidden in everything, it can be hard to avoid. Sticking to the basics of fruit, vegetables, dairy, and meat helps. In the ancient world, however, added sugars were rare. Honey was regarded as the sweetest of all substances. While our modern taste buds have been inundated with sugary delights, theirs would have known only very occasional fruits. So honey would especially have been a delight to the senses. Honey was also regarded as having healthy, wholesome, and healing properties. And it was seen as a high-energy source, sought after by Samson, Jonathan, and John the Baptist. It was given as a luxurious and prized gift (Genesis 43:11). So when Solomon the wise told us that God's wisdom is like honey, it dripped with meaning.

Earlier in the passage, he told his son not to envy the wicked (Proverbs 24:1). Their ways end in violence. And here Solomon contrasted that with the ways of the wise that provide "a future" and a "hope" that will "not be cut off." We hear in these words the similarity to the prophet Jeremiah, who would later say that God has plans for us, to bring us a hope and a future (Jeremiah 29:11). As we feed on God's Word, we can rest confident that God's ways are sweeter, healthier, and more prized than anything else. We can trust that this way of wisdom brings life, a future, and a hope for us and our families.

Satisfied

*"Buy wine and milk without money and
without price. Wherefore do ye spend money
for that which is not bread? and your labour
for that which satisfieth not? hearken diligently
unto me, and eat ye that which is good,
and let your soul delight itself in fatness."*
ISAIAH 55:1–2 KJV

Feeding babies and toddlers can be time-consuming and messy. Sometimes in our own quest for convenience, we want to simplify their diets by giving them convenience foods that aren't the healthiest. Let's face it; it can be hard to present them with a variety of healthy choices and clean up the applesauce and smooshed green peas from their hair or rice sprinkled over the side of the high chair. But variety is the name of the game in healthy eating, and also how the Bible chooses to communicate to us in food and drink metaphors to describe the Word, and later Christ the incarnate Word. Here in this passage in Isaiah, we have five consumable metaphors: water, wine, milk, bread, and "fatness." Just as we seek to round out our toddlers' diets, God seeks to round out our view of Him through such a variety.

Think through these metaphors a moment. Water is essential, necessary for life. Wine is a joy to the heart. Milk nourishes. And bread in their time was like water, a basic, essential sustenance. I chose the King James Version here because the more modern translations miss this extra-choice word—"fatness," a soul-satisfying abundance. The invitation here is to listen to the words of God and take them in as not only essential but joyful and satiating. Notice that there is no limitation put on the invitation. It is not "Take one." It is "Come and eat and drink until you want no more." There is plenty. Notice also that we are commanded to let our souls delight in the fare.

This passage is a foretaste of Christ's own invitation to come and drink living water and eat living bread. It reminds us that we are enjoined to delight in that which satisfies us completely.

What are some of your little one's favorite foods right now? What foods aren't tolerated?

_____

_____

_____

_____

_____

In the Isaiah 55:2 passage we studied in the last devotion, we are invited to delight our souls in the richest of fare. How does Jesus satisfy your soul, like the richest of foods?

_____

_____

_____

_____

_____

_____

How to Meditate
on the Word

*This Book of the Law shall not depart from
your mouth, but you shall meditate in it
day and night, that you may observe to
do according to all that is written in it.*
JOSHUA 1:8

Have you discovered some remedies yet for teething? Because the act
of chewing can offer some relief, pediatricians recommend freezing a
clean, wet washcloth and letting your toddler gnaw and suck on it. Or
they say you can offer frozen fruits, teething biscuits, and teething toys
built especially for those aching gums. As we continue thinking about
feeding on God's Word, we also can find relief by chewing on it repeatedly. We call this way of feeding on the Word meditating on it.

Meditating is not some mystical practice. In the biblical sense, it
means to think deeply, prayerfully, and slowly over a passage. While reading is like chewing and swallowing, meditating is more like chewing,
chewing, and chewing. With a toddler on the go, meditating on the Word
can be a good practice. You can write the verse on an index card and put
it in your pocket. Or take a picture of it with your cell phone. As you push
your little one on the swing, or as you take him on a walk with the stroller,
pull out the card or picture and read over this verse. Prayerfully ask God
how He wants you to apply it right now in your life. Or pray that verse
over your child. Let that verse linger with you and, as the book of Joshua
says, let it "not depart from your mouth," but "day and night" meditate
on it. Let God bring relief to your soul, as you—like a toddler—teethe on
His soothing words.

How Not to Consume the Word

If anyone is a hearer of the word and not a doer,
he is like a man observing his natural face in a
mirror; for he observes himself, goes away, and
immediately forgets what kind of man he was.

JAMES 1:23–24

By now your toddler has been eating table food for a while, but the training in eating is far from done, right? As the foods move from super soft to more challenging, over and over again we must encourage our little ones to chew and swallow carefully. We teach them to eat a balanced meal and eventually to say "please" and "thank you."

Likewise, as we think about how to feed on God's Word, there are dos and don'ts. Some of us listen to God's Word or read it mindlessly. We swallow without chewing or we simply cough it up. God says this is not the way to hear the Word. We are to be doers of the word, and not hearers only (James 1:28). We deceive ourselves if we think that simply hearing or reading the Word and doing nothing with it is of value. God says the Word should change us. When we look into it like a mirror, we should see ourselves more clearly. We should see where we need to change and ask for the Spirit's help to do it. Receiving the Word means that we should be receiving nourishment from it. It should cause good changes in us, just as eating foods high in calcium produces stronger bones and hair, while being malnourished would cause us to grow sick. Ask God today, "Is there any action or change You want me to make to live out Your words in my life?"

Memorize It

I have stored up your word in my heart,
that I might not sin against you.
PSALM 119:11 ESV

When I was about twelve, I memorized the entire book of James as part of a challenge put forth by our church's children's director. I was hungry for the Word, and God had blessed me with a good memory. I'm sorry to say I can't recite it all from memory today, but I still retain big chunks of it, along with many smaller portions from throughout the Bible that I've memorized recently or years ago.

Often these words come at times when I'm least expecting them. Sometimes when my eyes flutter open, there is a Word: "Let the morning bring me word of your unfailing love, for I have put my trust in you" (Psalm 143:8 NIV). Other times they come when I'm in the midst of hot tears or quaking with fear, like on a dark night stuck at a roadblock in East Africa: "Greater is he who is in [me] than he who is in the world" (1 John 4:4 NASB). And sometimes they come as correction: "Therefore, to him who knows to do good and does not do it, to him it is sin" (James 4:17).

I need these words. I need God speaking to me through them at these moments. If you've never memorized God's Word or if it's been a long time, let me encourage you to hide His Word in your heart. One of my favorite ways to do this since I've had little ones is to listen to some of the many excellent children's music recordings with verses set to music. (I've loved the groups Rain for Roots, Songs for Saplings, Slugs and Bugs, among others.) I've played these over and over again for my kids and have stored up words and truths in my heart and in theirs, because you don't know the day when you will need them nor how desperately you or someone else may need to have such words ready.

Describe a recent holiday you've celebrated with your toddler. What do you want to treasure about that day?

_____

_____

_____

_____

_____

_____

Write out a verse you have been meditating on or memorizing lately, or one that you want to think more deeply on or commit to memory. Why is this passage especially meaningful to you?

_____

_____

_____

_____

_____

_____

_____

Looking for the Wrong Bread

*"You seek Me, not because you saw the signs,
but because you ate of the loaves and were filled.
Do not labor for the food which perishes, but
for the food which endures to everlasting life."*
JOHN 6:26–27

Some days my toddler is constantly eating. He is like a hungry machine, and food is always on his mind. I guess some days I'm like that too.

Perhaps one of the reasons God chose to use the metaphor of feeding on His Word—and in the New Testament of feeding on Jesus, the incarnate Word—was because He knows food is often top of mind.

The five thousand who gathered to hear Christ speak near the Sea of Galilee were no different. Their tummies were rumbling, and that made it hard to concentrate. Jesus had compassion on them and fed them. But then the next day, when some of those five thousand crossed the sea in their boats to find Jesus again, He rebuked them: "You seek me, not because you saw the signs, but because you ate of the loaves and were filled." And He warned them that they'd come looking for the wrong kind of bread.

It's easy to get caught up in the here-and-now need, but Jesus reminds us that our greatest need is not something to satisfy our bellies but something to satisfy our souls. I find in my life it's easy to be discontent if I let myself focus on the things that I want and don't have. It's harder, but so much better if, rather than dwell in my discontent, I turn my eyes to Jesus. Spending time meditating on all the riches I have in Him—this fills me and changes me.

Jesus, the Bread of Life

"I am the living bread that came down from heaven. If anyone eats of this bread, he will live forever. And the bread that I will give for the life of the world is my flesh."
JOHN 6:51 ESV

In the Old Testament, David, Solomon, and the prophets talk about the Word, God's words, and the Law as something to feed upon. In the opening lines of the book of John, we hear God call Jesus the Word: "In the beginning was the Word, and the Word was with God, and the Word was God" (John 1:1). Jesus is God's Word incarnate, His living love letter to us. So it is fitting that in explaining to the hungry crowds that they needed spiritual nourishment, Jesus would call Himself the "Living Bread."

Bread to Jesus' audience was absolutely essential. From rich to poor, bread was the most common denominator of essential sustenance. It wasn't an add-on or an afterthought but the undeniable basic necessity of life, like water. It is no accident that Christ calls Himself the Living Water and the Bread of Life. He is essential—absolutely necessary—to life. As mamas, we know about essential foods for our toddlers. We would never let our little ones go without cow's milk, breastmilk, or some other calcium-rich alternative when their bodies are growing so fast. Likewise, we need to see the Word of God as absolutely essential to our daily lives. It's not something we can just skip and still be properly nourished. We need to feed on Jesus daily. Our lives as mamas can be busy, so be creative in this. Snack on His Word throughout the day: read it, listen to it, stream great sermons, or sing along with Christian music. However you do it, remember God's Word is essential sustenance for daily life.

Taste and See!

Oh, taste and see that the LORD is good;
blessed is the man who trusts in Him!
PSALM 34:8

Toddlers are notoriously picky eaters. My toddlers were the same, stubbornly refusing new foods that they found objectionable, often without so much as a taste. Recently my three-year-old adamantly declared his dislike for salmon. "But you haven't tried it!" chimed my whole tableful of salmon lovers. "Give it one little taste! It's so good. You'll love it if you try it," encouraged my eleven-year-old, whose favorite food, hands down, is salmon.

Here's the thing: When we've come to love something, we really want others to enjoy it also. It is part of our delight to share the delight with others. In this psalm, David had tasted and seen that the Lord is good, and he was asking others to taste-test His goodness. The word for *taste* here means to try the flavor of something (Job 12:11) or to eat just a little in order to understand what something is (1 Samuel 14:24, 29, 43; Jonah 3:7). If you know Jesus as the Living Bread, you can't help but want to recommend Him to others. You are outspoken—"Taste and see!"—because you have been so completely satisfied in Him. We can't force-feed others to try Jesus, but we can certainly be like my table full of testifiers: "Try this! You will LOVE it!" (By the way, the three-year-old loves salmon now!) Let us press on to recommend the Bread of Life to everyone we know.

Who is your toddler's favorite person to have for a visit? Is it a grandparent, a playmate, a neighbor? Why do you think your little one is drawn to that person?

_____

_____

_____

_____

_____

_____

_____

_____

How have you tasted and seen that Jesus is good in your life? Pray for someone for whom you long to see try Jesus.

_____

_____

_____

_____

_____

_____

_____

_____

An Invitation to Feast

"Then the master said to the servant, 'Go out into the highways and hedges, and compel them to come in, that my house may be filled.'"
LUKE 14:23

Have you ever sent out invitations to a party or let people know more informally that you were hosting an event and gotten loads of verbal commitments, only to have just a handful of people actually show up? It's frustrating. You've spent time, effort, and money preparing food, setting out decorations, and getting the house ready; maybe you've even rented a venue, only to be blown off. In the parable of the great supper told in Luke 14:15–24, the host has the same experience. And the excuses he gets are lame! Who tells you they are going to come to your party but forgets they are getting married the same day? Or who buys a piece of land or another major purchase and doesn't go see it beforehand? These people clearly don't value the host or the feast.

Jesus invites us daily to spend time in His Word, not only feasting on the goodness of His grace to us but fellowshipping in communion with Him. But all too often we blow Him off. We offer lame excuses or, worse, we just don't show up. We stay up too late binge-watching a favorite series or spend an hour on social media scrolling mindlessly and don't show up at His Word. Then we bemoan our lack of time. And we're cranky because we're spiritually hungry and relationally empty. Yes, you are a busy mama. Yes, you have a toddler to chase after. Yes, you have lots on your plate. But ask Jesus to help you see His invitation for what it is: not a burden but an unimaginable delight—a feast. Ask Him to help you not to make excuses, but for Him to help you make it to the table. He will answer in ways beyond your imagination.

A Fore"taste"

*As they were eating, Jesus took bread, blessed
and broke it, and gave it to the disciples
and said, "Take, eat; this is My body."*
MATTHEW 26:26

Times of sweet fellowship around the table—maybe they aren't as frequent these days now that you have a busy toddler. But likely, you've had some kind of taste, however imperfect, of a good meal with close friends around the table. Jesus did too. And at the Last Supper, we see the culmination of several metaphors: from the manna in the wilderness (Exodus 16), to the honey of God's commands (Psalm 119:103), to Isaiah's invitation to eat freely (Isaiah 55:1), to Jesus' declaration of being Living Bread and Living Water (John 4:14–15; 6:51; 7:37–38). Here we have Jesus, the Word-made-flesh, inviting us to feast. He is provision in our wilderness, sweetness to our senses, living and everlasting satiety. He invites us freely to accept His sacrifice on our behalf that we might know eternal life and fellowship.

From time eternal, the Father, Son, and Holy Spirit have enjoyed perfect joy and love in their relationship. Sin barred us from fellowship with God. But now when the Scriptures tell us of the table of our Lord in this last meal, we catch an imperfect glimpse through this flawed, ragtag band of followers of that perfect fellowship to come. Jesus invites us to join in this fore"taste" on a regular basis, accepting His sacrifice, remembering Him, but also looking forward to the day when by grace we will join in this fellowship feast to beat all feasts. In fact, Jesus said to them, "But I say to you, I will not drink of this fruit of the vine from now on until that day when I drink it new with you in My Father's kingdom" (Matthew 26:29 NIV). Hallelujah, that day is coming!

A Feast of Nations

*In this mountain the LORD of hosts will
make for all people a feast of choice pieces, a
feast of wines on the lees, of fat things full of
marrow, of well-refined wines on the lees.*
ISAIAH 25:6

B y now you've celebrated all the major holidays with your little one, but what fun it is as they begin to be able to partake in the feast. Whether it's a baby-sized sampling of turkey and stuffing, the Easter ham and sides, or that favorite Fourth of July picnic spread, it's fun to share the joy of the holiday with them. But these joys in sharing the table are but mere foretastes of the wonder of sharing the feast to come. Here Isaiah foretold it: a feast of nations—a lavish banquet. Jesus revisited the theme: He talked of a banquet (Luke 14:15–24) and also a wedding feast (Matthew 22:1–14). Those you would expect to be there were not, but the poor, the lame, the crippled, the outsider, those on the wayside—all were invited. There would not be an empty place at the table. Jesus raised His glass again to the coming fulfillment of this metaphor (26:29). And then in Revelation, John gave us a sneak peak of the marriage supper of the Lamb and His bride (Revelation 19:6–9). John wrote, "Then I heard what seemed to be the voice of a great multitude, like the roar of many waters and like the sound of mighty peals of thunder, crying out, 'Hallelujah! For the Lord our God the Almighty reigns'" (Revelation 19:6 ESV).

What a privilege it is to be invited to this feast to come! In fact, the angel said, "Write this: Blessed are those who are invited" (v. 9 ESV). He wanted us to remember that we have been blessed to even receive an invitation! And what a privilege it is to invite others. God desires worshippers from every tribe, tongue, and nation—and we get the awesome honor of sharing this with anyone and everyone. Oh, that they would not turn down a seat!

What outings have you and your toddler taken lately? Does he or she have a favorite place to go with you?

_____

_____

_____

_____

_____

Often during communion we are told to look back and remember Christ's sacrifice. While this is very important, it is also important to take a future look at the joy that awaits us in heaven. How does this future hope motivate you?

_____

_____

_____

_____

_____

_____

SEVEN
Speaking

Your Eighteen-Month-Old,

Developmental Guide

Hello, independence! You may be noticing that your toddler's favorite word these days is no and that he is dead set on doing things his way. Try not to be offended. This is actually a good sign; your little one is growing in independence and seeing himself as a separate person with his own thoughts and ideas. Support the new confidence, while also teaching him to speak kindly if his ideas are different from yours. You want your little one to revel in his autonomy, but you also want to always inculcate an attitude of respect in your home.

Not only is your toddler most likely showing signs of more independence, you may also be noticing a lot of newfound confidence these days. All that walking, running, and climbing may be giving her a boost of self-assurance.

While independence and confidence may be growing, so too may those epic temper tantrums. How can you help them navigate these big emotions? First, you may notice that a lot of these tantrums occur at the most inconvenient times. Like when you are trying to get out the door or have a cart full of groceries at the checkout. Sometimes tantrums occur because your child is feeling overwhelmed or overloaded. They may also happen when you aren't able to give them your focus or attention. Help sidestep the tantrum by giving yourself an extra fifteen minutes to get out the door or making sure your child has a snack or nap before that grocery trip.

When tantrums do occur, try to help him put words to his emotions and attempt to stay calm yourself. "I see you are feeling angry that Mommy said no to candy right now," or "I see how sad you are that your toy broke. It makes me sad that you're sad. Can I give you a hug?" Helping him put words to his feelings will help make those feelings less overwhelming and help him grow in his emotional intelligence.

Your little one has most likely transitioned to one longer nap (perhaps about two hours) in the afternoon, as well as about a twelve-hour stretch at night. Sometimes children about this age have a little trouble getting to sleep. Try to be consistent in the bedtime routine and let him fall asleep on his own. The self-soothing while going to sleep will help him learn to self-soothe if he wakes in the middle of the night as well.

Finally, you may notice your little one eats ravenously one day and barely touches her food the next. Not to worry, inconsistency in eating is common among toddlers. Keep offering three meals a day, two snacks, and about three to four (eight-ounce) cups of milk or nursing sessions if you are still breastfeeding.

Developmental Focus: Speaking

Your child has been absorbing language since the time she first heard your voice in utero. For the first year of life and usually about half of the second, most of a child's language development is what experts call "receptive language," and it's a crucial part of language development. What is she learning through all this listening? She is storing up vocabulary and unconsciously internalizing many rules of grammar, as well as noticing body language and inflection as she gets ready for the speaking stage.

It's good to keep in mind that there is a wide range of normal in language development, like other developmental milestones. By eighteen months, most toddlers can say about ten words. About 50 percent can say twenty or more. If she hasn't already, soon your child may begin stringing two-word phrases together, and instead of just pointing to an item she wants, she will begin asking for it by name. For a while your toddler may be adding about two to three spoken words a month, but there usually comes a point when there is something of a language growth spurt, when suddenly your child will add more like ten to twelve words in a month and begin being much more expressive.

The more verbal you are with your child, the more likely he or she will follow your cues. Narrating everyday activities, introducing objects and people by name, and encouraging repetition are ways you can help your toddler blossom with language development.

Just as your toddler is growing in his ability to speak, as Christians we are also growing in our ability to speak in ways that honor God and avoid those habits of speech that dishonor Him. The Bible has so much to say about how we speak and what kinds of things God wants us to speak about. Let's dive in and spend some time meditating on how we can honor God with our words.

The Source of Our Speech

"A good man out of the good treasure of his heart brings forth good; and an evil man out of the evil treasure of his heart brings forth evil. For out of the abundance of the heart his mouth speaks."
LUKE 6:45

As your toddler grows, he or she will be imitating your words—not just *what* you speak but *how* you speak. If you are habitually angry, you will hear it in how your little one speaks to you and others. If you are often irritable and complaining, your child's speech will grow to sound like your own. If you speak frequently with disrespect or contempt, buckle your seatbelt for the teen years—it's going to be a rough ride.

All of us sin in our speech. However, if we are growing in Christ, the way we speak should be transforming. But here's the deal: trying to work on just our words is not really going to work. We have to begin with our hearts. Jesus tells us that our words are the overflow of our hearts. So if you are spewing anger, gossip, or unkindness, it's like a check engine light going off on the dashboard. You *need* to open the hood and see what's going on. Simply talk to God about it: "Lord, I really sound irritated today. Can You help me figure out what's bothering me?" If you make a habit of listening to *how* you are speaking to others and taking the heart issues that you discover to God in prayer, you will find Him bringing the kind of change you need: heart change.

Flaming Arrows

*Like a madman who throws firebrands,
arrows, and death, is the man who deceives
his neighbor, and says, "I was only joking!"*
PROVERBS 26:18–19

My husband and I *love* to joke. We playfully tease each other a lot! His sense of humor was one of the things that first drew me to him. And you can imagine that now as we raise our boys, we also have a house full of laughter. Joking, being silly, and good-humored teasing are part of what makes our home ours. I believe God loves laughter. But He also gives us a warning about *how* we joke with one another. We are never to use "I was only joking" as a cover for speaking unkind words that come from an unkind heart. Our culture is often guilty of this. We hear it in the cynicism of sitcoms, the biting edge of our news commentators, and the abrasiveness that passes for humor in too many of our get-togethers.

Your toddler will grow up within the verbal atmosphere of your home. So thinking about how you speak to one another is so important. In our home, even when I tease my husband or my children, I never want to say something in a joking way that might actually be hurtful. I'd never hand my boys flaming arrows for backyard shooting practice. Likewise, we realize speech is powerful, and some words can set your whole house ablaze. Thinking about the verbal atmosphere of your home is one of the best ways you can help your child grow to be a person whose speech is seasoned with grace, goodness, and truth. And even though their vocabulary is limited now, they are picking up much more than we realize. As followers of Christ and as parents, let our homes overflow with the healthy kind of laughter, not the hurtful kind.

Speaking the Truth in Love

We should no longer be children . . . but,
speaking the truth in love, may grow up in all
things into Him who is the head—Christ.
EPHESIANS 4:14–15

As we continue thinking about the verbal atmosphere of our homes, and the kind of environment our toddlers will grow within, let's talk about marriage for a moment. Conflict is inevitable. Healthy marriages have conflict too. That should be a given. If you are married, and you and your spouse disagree, it does not mean you are doing something wrong. You are two distinct people; iron will sharpen iron, and sometimes there will be sparks. But as you disagree, let your tongues be ruled by truth and love. When truth isn't spoken, someone is usually stuffing something down inside. This can come back as bitterness or contempt if we aren't careful. Yes, sometimes we are called to bear with one another (Ephesians 4:2) and overlook one another's offenses (Proverbs 19:11). There is definitely great wisdom in this. But many times God *is* calling you to speak.

Which brings us to the second part of this command: speak the truth *in love*. We need to speak up at the right time and in the right way. Before you speak, pray about it. Ask God if it is something He wants you to overlook or talk about. If He wants you to speak up, pray for an opportune moment in private. And pray for your own motivation to be that of love. It's easy to criticize to make ourselves feel better or because we are focused on our comfort. It's hard to speak truth in love—because we want the best for someone, even if we must first walk through the tension and pain of saying hard things to get there. Working on our marriages may seem hard, but truth be told, you can do nothing better for your toddler.

What words are in your toddler's vocabulary these days? How else does he or she communicate with you?

_____

_____

_____

_____

_____

_____

_____

_____

_____

Which comes easier for you, speaking the truth or speaking in love? Write a prayer for God's help in doing both.

_____

_____

_____

_____

_____

_____

_____

_____

An Apt Word

*A word fitly spoken is like apples
of gold in settings of silver.*
PROVERBS 25:11

Your toddler's vocabulary is so limited at this point that even if she has a range of words, chances are she may call her fork a spoon or her knee a nose. It makes life entertaining, for sure, to hear what they'll say next. While we are happy with whatever our toddlers can communicate, for us, expectations are just a bit higher. We all know our words are important, but it's not just the right words we aim for, but the right words at the right time in the right way. This involves a lot. To speak the right words, we must cultivate a heart of wisdom. We must soak in God's words and principles such that His truths and not the world's are what are ready on our minds and tongues.

Next, we have to be listening. We must listen to the person to whom we are speaking—not just to their words but to what those words reveal about their deeper spiritual needs. And we must listen to the Holy Spirit. *Does God want me to open my mouth right now or keep listening to my friend vent?* and *God, help me know what my husband needs in this moment.* Or *What words of reassurance is God wanting me to speak to my child's heart as we sit together today?*

So there's wisdom, listening to the one before us, and listening to the Spirit, and finally there is love. We must ask, "How do I say this in a way that this person can hear?" Jesus used all manners of speaking: He was direct with some people, used figurative language with others, was sometimes brief and other times lengthy, but in everything He was guided by love, even when He had to speak a word of rebuke.

Know Thy Audience

We urge you, brothers and sisters,
warn those who are idle and disruptive,
encourage the disheartened, help the
weak, be patient with everyone.
1 THESSALONIANS 5:14 NIV

Your little one just tossed her snack cup to the floor and scattered Cheerios everywhere. She is crying and about to throw herself on the floor because it's past bedtime and she is exhausted. Quick quiz: Is this a good time to talk in detail about why we don't throw food on the floor? Probably not.

Have you ever tried to give your toddler detailed instructions during a meltdown on how you want them to behave? How'd that go? Even though I'm not new to this rodeo of toddler parenting, I still find myself getting it wrong at times. I give a lecture when the little one just needs me to carry him to bed and talk about it tomorrow when he's rested. Or I treat my older child like he's lazy when he really is just frustrated and has stopped his math work because he does not understand. Part of having an apt word is knowing the needs of those whom God puts before you. It's knowing when their bodies and minds can handle what.

God instructs us to warn people who are "idle and disruptive, encourage the disheartened, [and] help the weak." He does not want us to warn the weak or help the idle. Do you see? It's the right response for the right need and the discernment to know the difference.

Please and Thank You

One of them, when he saw that he was healed,
returned, and with a loud voice glorified God,
and fell down on his face at His feet, giving
Him thanks. And he was a Samaritan.
LUKE 17:15–16

Aside from "mama" and "dada," one of my toddler's first words was "please." It's a sweet reflection of something we say a lot in our family. "Please" and "thank you" are reflections of what we really value: gratitude and kindness. I'm a firm believer that with enough repetition, such simple courtesies can become lifelong habits, and what a difference they make, not only to the hearer but also to the one saying the words. It may sound obvious, but my husband and I often say "please" and "thank you" to each other; we notice the dignity and love it infuses in ordinary tasks. It communicates value, especially in the closest relationships, where we too often take people who serve us most for granted.

Clearly, Jesus values gratitude. In this story of the ten lepers who were healed in Luke 17:11–19, we see that while ten were healed, only one came back to say thank you. It's a fascinating story. I like especially that the lepers were healed not in Jesus' presence but on the way, as they obeyed. Notice also in verse 13 that when they saw Jesus, they lifted up their voices with a loud cry. And then notice in verses 15 and 16 how the Samaritan gave thanks with a loud voice. May the fever and pitch of our pleas match or be outmatched by the fever and pitch of our praise!

Finally, sometimes gratitude may take us out of our way; it may cost us time and effort, or even delay gratification, but it comes with spiritual benefit. God was magnified, and Jesus Himself pronounced blessing over the man. Let our words drip with thankfulness.

What are your little one's favorite board books these days?

_____

_____

_____

_____

_____

_____

_____

_____

_____

What has God done lately in your life? For what do you need to stop and take a moment to thank Him? Write a prayer of thankfulness here.

_____

_____

_____

_____

_____

_____

_____

_____

Hard Words

*Brothers and sisters, if someone is caught
in a sin, you who live by the Spirit should
restore that person gently. But watch
yourselves, or you also may be tempted.*
GALATIANS 6:1 NIV

As mamas to little ones, we will have to say no more than we'd ever
care to do. We'll have to be the bad guy, the one who comes between our
toddler and all kinds of mischief and danger and sometimes fun. It can
get wearisome being the one to say no. And unfortunately, it can also be
something that causes us to stumble.

Even though we are correcting a toddler, we very much need Paul's
words to the Galatians to remind us of a few important points of caution.

First, notice that Paul was speaking to people who "live by the Spirit."
That means that loving confrontation—even with our toddler—happens
in the context of being led by God's Spirit. As you are led by the Spirit,
sometimes God may direct you to correct your child lovingly, pointing
out right from wrong, modeling the right, and explaining the wrong. At
other times, the Spirit may lead you just to redirect your toddler or simply
let something go (Proverbs 19:11).

Galatians 6:1 also reminds us that the goal of such confrontation is
restoration. We don't confront to shame or to punish. We don't discipline
even for the sake of well-behaved children. We confront in order to help
that person get into right relationship with God.

Over all this, God calls us to speak with gentleness. Gentleness goes
hand in hand with the command to watch ourselves. You see, when we
know that we, too, are sinners, we restore with gentleness because we
know how much we also need grace.

Words of Confession

*When I kept silent, my bones wasted away
through my groaning all day long. For day
and night your hand was heavy on me; my
strength was sapped as in the heat of summer.*
PSALM 32:3–4 NIV

As we continue thinking about our speech this month, I want to focus on confession. As new Christians, we began with repentance and belief. The funny thing is that as we progress as Christians on this side of eternity, we never get past our need for repentance and belief. As God convicts us of sin, He will also move us to confess—to Him and often to the person we've wronged. As moms, we are going to fail our kids often. One of the best things we can model for them is confession, repentance, and a request for forgiveness.

Do you want your future teen son to come to you when he's messed up or your future grade school daughter to confess the lie she's just told you? If you do, begin modeling early confession, repentance, and asking for forgiveness. It can be simple: "I'm sorry, sweetie, Mommy should not have raised her voice at you. I was feeling upset and I took it out on you. That was wrong. Can you please forgive me?"

When we fail to confess our sins to God and one another, something inside us wastes away. Next time, it becomes a little harder to confess and a little easier to rationalize our actions. Little by little our hearts get hard. Be outspoken in your need for grace, and you will create a culture of forgiveness.

Words of Forgiveness

*Be kind and compassionate to one
another, forgiving each other, just
as in Christ God forgave you.*
EPHESIANS 4:32 NIV

Have you forgiven your toddler today? That may be a totally new thought to you. But as parents we are going to not only have to ask our children to forgive us a lot, but we are also going to need to forgive them. We'll need to forgive them for the ways they hurt us willfully and the ways they hurt us inadvertently. As they grow, their ability to bless us grows, but so, too, does their ability to wound. In many ways, you will be the face of forgiveness to them until they are old enough to understand God's forgiveness. The offenses will often be small—the crayon scribble on the wall or "Me no like Mommy"—but sometimes they will be large. Either way it's important that you model a forgiving heart toward your little one now and as he grows.

One of the ways I see this fail to work in our lives as parents is when our kids commit a series of smaller misbehaviors and our irritation with them grows. Pretty soon we find ourselves losing our cool and overreacting. But if we took the time to gently correct the smaller offenses and speak our forgiveness over them, we'd also do a better job of not letting that bitterness that rankles inside us grow. Speak the words "I forgive you" and model a reconciling embrace, and it will pay dividends for their spiritual and relational lives in the future.

Does your toddler have a morning routine? What's a favorite morning you've spent lately with him or her?

_____

_____

_____

_____

_____

_____

_____

Do you find it easier to ask forgiveness or give forgiveness? Write a prayer asking for God's help in the area that's harder for you.

_____

_____

_____

_____

_____

_____

_____

Words of Testimony

Let each generation tell its children of your
mighty acts; let them proclaim your power.
PSALM 145:4 NLT

When my mom was three and a half years old, she contracted polio. She woke up one morning with a fever and her right leg paralyzed. It was a terrifying epidemic at that time. My mom was quarantined at a hospital several hours from home and could only see her parents once a week for an hour. Round-the-clock penicillin shots increased the horror she experienced. The story is long, but the brief version is that when my grandparents were turned away from the leading medical facility at the time for the treatment of polio, they pulled their little pickup truck off to the side of the road and prayed. Around the very same time that they prayed, a state away where my mom languished in her hospital bed, she started to get movement back in her leg. My grandparents received a call from an astonished doctor when they got home.

My mom recounted to me many times the story of God's healing and how she learned to walk again. She taught me other everyday stories of God's faithfulness to her. Gradually, the legacy of God's work in her life became a part of my own story. Like the verse above, Psalm 78:4 (NLT) says, "We will not hide these truths from our children; we will tell the next generation about the glorious deeds of the LORD." We have a duty to God to tell our children about His goodness. Start now and don't stop. Let your story become a part of theirs.

Words of Discipleship

"You shall teach them diligently to your children, and shall talk of them when you sit in your house, when you walk by the way, when you lie down, and when you rise up."
DEUTERONOMY 6:7

Oh sweet mama friends, we come to the words that are my heartbeat for you. This is why I've written these devotionals, and it is what I pray for you. How I long that we would pour this into our children. And by pour into them I don't mean obsess about decorating their big-boy rooms, buying those cute outfits, or figuring out the best preschool or extracurricular choices. What I mean is that we would spend ourselves that they might know God and His Word and ways *deeply*.

Perhaps your little one has only a handful of words and a comically unsteady gait, but it's not too early to begin this lifelong journey of discipleship. Teach her to pray. Model praying when she rises, when she goes to sleep, when she eats, when there is a need, or when there is a cause for gladness. Sing songs about God. Let her earliest songs be memories of His love. Read stories of God's great works or retell the stories in your own words. Act out David and Goliath or Noah and his ark or Jesus and the fish and loaves. Let God's ways be on your lips when you sit, walk, lie down, or rise up. Don't stop telling, modeling, and dialoguing with your child about this relationship you have with the living God. Begin, Mama, and be diligent to the end.

Words of Evangelism

Sanctify the Lord God in your hearts,
and always be ready to give a defense to
everyone who asks you a reason for the hope
that is in you, with meekness and fear.
1 PETER 3:15

When I was a kid, it seemed like there was never a repairman who entered our house who didn't somehow end up in a spiritually deep conversation with my mom. It wasn't forced or abrasive but always natural somehow. When I was in grade school, I remember helping my dad practice sharing his faith as he went through some training at church on it. I would give all the wrong answers so he'd have to work harder. And when I was old enough to memorize Scripture, I learned key verses that summarize what it is to believe in Christ. From a young age, sharing our faith was a part of my family's DNA. Many a Sunday or holiday our table was set with extra places as the lonely joined us for a meal. My parents weren't preachers or missionaries, just everyday Christians who modeled an open heart of hospitality. I treasure this.

As you raise your toddler, will telling others about your faith be a part of your family DNA? Will your child overhear you telling others about the reason for your hope? Will your child learn along with your family to be an ambassador for Christ and make sacrifices big and small for the gospel (2 Corinthians 5:20)? You may have only a toddler, but your habits and the culture of your home are already beginning. Create an atmosphere of gospel hospitality. Look for those times and places where you can extend an invitation, start a conversation, and be a winsome witness of the hope you have.

Does your toddler have a favorite song he likes for you to sing or likes to hear? What does your little one do these days when he hears music?

_____

_____

_____

_____

_____

_____

_____

Brainstorm about your vision for building discipleship and evangelism into the culture of your home. What short-term and long-term ideas do you have? What fits with the gifts God has given you and your spouse?

_____

_____

_____

_____

_____

_____

EIGHT
Creating

Your Nineteen-Month-Old,

Developmental Guide

Your toddler is really blossoming day by day into a big boy or girl. Around this time you may notice a sudden liftoff in vocabulary or creativity. Physical movement is coming more easily. And your little one may even show signs of readiness for potty training (or they may hold off for quite a while—that's fine too!).

While his or her skills are expanding day by day, you may also be thinking about or already be in the throes of expanding the size of your family. If you are planning on adding to your family, it's always good to start preparing your little one for the idea of a new sibling ahead of time. You could buy a baby doll and practice ways of being gentle with "his" baby or cut out and paste pictures together of things babies need.

Speaking of babies, your little one may be about triple the size she was at birth. According to the World Health Organization, an average nineteen-month-old girl weighs 23.9 pounds and stands 32.2 inches tall, while the average boy weighs 24.6 pounds and stands 32.8 inches tall.

While you are making sure your growing son or daughter gets what he or she needs for that growing body, make sure you are also taking care to avoid things that they don't need: like too much screen time. Doctors say children between eighteen and twenty-four months should get less than an hour of screen time a day. If you are watching television, try to make sure the show is educational and talk about it with your little one. Developmentally, though, it's good to keep those screens off. Your toddler needs to explore new experiences, not zone out and let someone else do the exploring.

Sleep needs are staying the same this month, with twelve to fourteen hours of sleep usually split into one longer nap and nighttime sleep. Staying consistent with the bedtime and nap-time routine can help if your child is showing resistance to napping or sleeping. Continue offering a variety of nutritious foods with three meals, two to three snacks, and several cups of milk (or nursing sessions) a day.

Developmental Focus: Play

Play is an absolutely crucial part of your toddler's "work" of learning about her world. Physically, mentally, socially, and emotionally, your toddler is learning so much through the simple act of playing. Here are some ways you can encourage this work.

Ideas for physical play:

- Balls to kick, toss, push, and roll
- Push toys and pull toys
- Tunnels to crawl through
- Blocks or cups to nest or stack
- Chunky wooden puzzles

- Tip: First let your child explore toys like the above on her own to see how they work. Later, show her new ways to use the toys.

Ideas for social and verbal play:

- Ring-around-the-rosy or chase
- A pretend telephone to "talk" to relatives or friends
- Plenty of playdates and park time with other kids
- Tip: Model words for playing nicely with others.

Ideas for sensory play:

- Sandbox or water table
- Musical instruments
- Clay
- Tip: Sensory play can be messy. Take the items outside if possible and store in airtight containers out of reach when not in use. This will cut down on the mess.

At nineteen months your little one is all about understanding his world through play. For him, play is both a way of joy and a way of work. It is a way to learn about his world. We, too, have been made to play and enjoy this world God has put us in. We've also been made to create and cultivate. This month, we'll focus on our creative God and how He has made work and play good, as well as rest. We'll think about our motive and our hope for creation and cultivation.

God's Creative Variety and Wisdom

How many are your works, LORD!
In wisdom you made them all; the
earth is full of your creatures.
PSALM 104:24 NIV

One of the delights of parenthood is seeing the wonders of the natural world with renewed eyes in the wonder of our children. I have loved watching my toddler giggle at the feel of the water tickling his toes at the lake, and I've enjoyed seeing his nose pressed against the glass as he looks at snowflakes coming down. In every season there is a wonder to behold and the variety of God's creativity all around.

Challenge yourself to get down on your child's level and look at the world. If it's warm, go outside and walk barefoot in the grass with your toddler. Notice the variety of living things, from dandelions to daffodils, from woolly caterpillars to roly-polies. Stop and see what grabs your little one's attention. Or if it's chilly, bundle up and head out. Maybe you'll crunch leaves or snow underfoot. Maybe you can catch a snowflake on your tongue and remember with awe that no two are the same. Whatever the season, your little one will help you see the wonder afresh, and you can help them see the fingerprints of God in it all. Whether it's the dazzling color and variety of fall leaves, the gorgeous hues of shells at the sea, the baffling assortment of animals at the zoo, or the delicious range of produce at the market, we can help our children see how God delighted in the very act of making, and they can help us experience the wonder afresh with all our senses.

God's Creative Diversity

After this I looked, and behold, a great multitude that no one could number, from every nation, from all tribes and peoples and languages, standing before the throne and before the Lamb.

REVELATION 7:9 ESV

Not only did God delight in making variety when it came to plants, animals, rocks, and planets, but He delighted in doing the same in the apex of His creation: humans. The idea of loving every race and tribe isn't a modern idea; it's God's idea! In Revelation, we have a picture of the massive variety of peoples assembled before the throne of God praising Him. People from every tribe and tongue and nation, a sea of beautiful diversity united in their worship of the one true and living God.

We also see a beautiful diversity in the way God makes each of us so absolutely unique. No two people, not even identical twins, share the same fingerprints or the same giftings.

You can point out to your toddler today how beautifully unique God has made her. Teach her that even though someone may have the same name or the same hair color, no one on earth is exactly like her. Rejoice with your toddler in this uniqueness and in your own. Thank God that we can reflect His love of diversity as we are each so special, and that we can reflect His love of unity as together we join to glorify Him forever.

God's Creative Purpose

For we are His workmanship, created in Christ
Jesus for good works, which God prepared
beforehand that we should walk in them.
EPHESIANS 2:10

It only takes a short stroll through the woods or an evening of stargazing to marvel in the variety and joy God found in creating. His wisdom and diversity in creation are not hidden. But what was God's purpose in all this creative energy? Why did He go to the trouble of creating at all—especially if He knew that we would betray Him?

The answer is both simple and profound: for His own glory. Every detail of the created order was made to bring Him glory. And when He redeemed us, He also did it for His own glory. We are, as Paul called us, God's "workmanship," or His *poiema* in the Greek—His masterpiece, His poem, His work of art. Do you ever sit back and just marvel at the wonder and beauty of your toddler? How her little legs work together to walk, how she is learning words and gaining so many new skills each day? There is a reason you stop to marvel: your toddler is a "poiema"—a masterpiece of God's making. And you are too! We bring glory to God in the mastery and magnificence of how He made us.

We also bring God glory through the good works we do—works that He has prepared for us to walk in. You were created to do good to bring Him glory. God is not selfish in this pursuit of glory. He alone in the universe is right to pursue His glory because He alone deserves *all glory*.

How has your toddler helped you see the wonder of the world afresh with new eyes to marvel? Does his face light up with joy at a balloon tossed in the air, or does he let out a giggle as he splashes in a puddle? Give praise to God for the way our little ones help us to experience joy.

_____

_____

_____

_____

_____

_____

How has God uniquely gifted you? Is it hard to see yourself as His poiema—His poem, His masterpiece, His beautiful work of art? Praise God for His handiwork in making you.

_____

_____

_____

_____

_____

_____

_____

The Goodness of Work

Then the LORD God took the man and put him in the garden of Eden to tend and keep it.
GENESIS 2:15

Each one of my children loved to play "work" when they were toddlers. They loved the toy kitchen. They loved the toy tools. They loved to pretend to build or work in the garden. There is a reason we are drawn to work even from a very young age, and that is because work itself is good; God made work before the fall. God made us to love work—work itself is not an evil but a good. Work gives meaning and purpose to our days. Whether you are a stay-at-home mom or juggling work outside the home and a family, your work matters.

But don't get me wrong, God hasn't made us *only* for work, and we need a balance of work and rest and play. Since the fall, work has been filled with thorns and thistles. These represent how work has been plagued by frustrations and futilities. But that does not take away from the fact that God has designed us to create and cultivate. That means He made us to take joy in making, tending, preserving, and bringing order to the world around us. The psalmist said, "When you eat the fruit of the labor of your hands, you will be happy and it will go well for you" (Psalm 128:2 NASB 1995). There is a fitting joy in work. Teach your little one that God has made us to love to create and cultivate. Encourage their play now, and their joy in creating as they grow, by modeling a love of it yourself and a balance in keeping work and rest in their proper places.

The Goodness of Play

*"Of every tree of the garden you may
freely eat; but of the tree of the knowledge
of good and evil you shall not eat."*
GENESIS 2:16–17

Does your toddler hand you objects now with an expectation that you will pretend or play with her? A toy cup for you to sip? A baby doll for you to rock? A car to zoom across the ground? It's amazing to see this beautiful instinct to play that God has sown into our children. It is one of the wonders of parenting to watch them play and through them to be invited to enjoy our own playfulness again.

Yesterday we talked about how God made us to work, but it is also true that God made us to play. Sometimes work and play are hard to distinguish, especially when we are doing something we love. The Bible doesn't often use the word *play*, but it talks often of enjoyment, and even more often implies that enjoyment. For instance, in the command to Adam and Eve above, we usually focus on the prohibition—the Thou Shalt Not—and miss something obvious: God has created every other tree in this beautiful garden for Adam and Eve to enjoy. Play and delight go hand in hand. You will see it in the joy and wonder of your child popping a bubble or laughing in the bonding tussle of a tickle fight. One of the great reminders of the goodness of God is that He has made us to enjoy Him and this world. Let us never be too old to miss the sweetness of this.

The Goodness of Rest

The sleep of a laboring man is sweet,
whether he eats little or much.
ECCLESIASTES 5:12

We've spent a lot of time in this devotional thinking about a theology of rest, so I won't dwell too much on it here, except to emphasize that hard work and hard play help us to appreciate the goodness of rest even more. We've pondered this week how God has made us for work—with a desire to create and cultivate. We've lingered over how He has made us for play—with the capacity to delight in and enjoy the things He has made. And it is fitting that we also consider how He has made us for rest. The challenge of work makes rest all the more pleasant. We rest at the end of each day, relaxing into His ability to care for us even as we sleep. And when we really lean hard into the rhythms of how God has designed our week, keeping a holy rhythm of resting on our Sabbath day, we will find a deeply satisfying sweetness.

I sometimes imagine God standing back from the easel of creation at the end of each day and savoring what He had done. "It is good!" He didn't incessantly work. He took time to stop, reflect, and enjoy. Our toddlers are good at reminding us of our human need for rest. They need naps. They need periods of quiet play. They need lots of sleep at night. We can learn from them that God made us with similar needs for a rhythm of hard work, fun play, and satisfying rest.

What is your little one's favorite playtime activity these days?
How does he or she invite you to join?

_____

_____

_____

_____

_____

_____

_____

_____

Which do you find easiest to do: work, play, or rest? Write a
prayer asking God for His help in those areas that you naturally
tend to neglect.

_____

_____

_____

_____

_____

_____

_____

_____

Consecrated for Our Callings

He has filled them with skill to do all manner
of work of the engraver and the designer
and the tapestry maker, in blue, purple,
and scarlet thread, and fine linen, and
of the weaver—those who do every work
and those who design artistic works.
EXODUS 35:35

Have you ever considered that your particular skills and personality were gifted to you by God for His purposes? Sometimes motherhood feels overwhelming. But when you stop to realize that God gave you your particular child and put you in your particular place and time for a reason, it fills you with hope that you can do what He's called you to do.

When God called Jeremiah, He told him, "Before I formed you in the womb I knew you, and before you were born I consecrated you" (Jeremiah 1:5 ESV). Jeremiah had a special job as a prophet, but I believe God sets us apart for our particular callings as well. I say "callings" because we are all called to be creators and cultivators in a variety of ways across our lifetimes. Yes, sometimes He gives us a particular vocation, but even within that, sometimes things shift with time. And all of us are called to a variety of roles. For those reading, you are called to the role of mother, and perhaps also wife, many to the role of daughter, sister, or friend, in addition to your other creative and cultivating work. Wherever God has called you, take heart to know that He has filled you with skill and consecrated you with purpose.

Guided by His Glory

*So whether you eat or drink or whatever
you do, do it all for the glory of God.*
1 CORINTHIANS 10:31 NIV

From the beginning we can teach our children that there is no division between the sacred and the secular. Sunday is not simply the day for God, while all the other days are days for "normal life." By no means! Every day, every activity, every thought and moment can be lived unto Him and for His glory.

There once was a monk named Brother Lawrence. He wrote a short book called *The Practice of the Presence of God*. In it he describes how it was in his time as an ordinary dishwasher in the monastery that he really learned that all things—even the most menial task, like washing dishes—could be transformed into spiritual acts of worship if approached with the right attitude. We model this for our children daily by how we approach our ordinary work. Our attitude can be a begrudging one as we change a diaper, fix a meal, or meet with a client, or it can be an attitude of service to Jesus and worship of Him. We can perform our ordinary tasks as our Lord prayed "on earth as it is in heaven" with joy, with worship, and with purpose, and we can teach our children to do the same, whether it's doing a small chore like picking up their toys or something creative like coloring a picture. Let everything we do be all for the glory of God!

Play with Me

*[Jesus] emptied himself, by taking the form of
a servant, being born in the likeness of men.*
PHILIPPIANS 2:7 ESV

I was at the sink doing dishes when my three-year-old begged, "Play with me, Mama." I felt like a horrible mother for feeling it, but at that moment, I didn't want to play. I wanted to muscle through my to-do list. I wanted the sink tidied, the food put away, and to see my face reflecting in a clean countertop. I didn't feel like playing.

The request came again later that morning when I'd just dumped the mound of clothes from the dryer onto the bed to fold: "Mama, play with me!" Finally, I realized it wasn't my three-year-old interrupting me. God was interrupting me. How could I expect this little one to obey unless I've first gotten down on his level and entered into his world? He wants my presence amidst blocks, trains, and construction trucks. He wants me hiding in his fort, building a tunnel, busting out the finger paints, and getting my own hands into the glorious mess with him. This bending low is what Jesus did when He came to earth as an infant: He bent low into my humanity, He entered into my world. He didn't stand far off but got down on my level. Sometimes being the mom who finds herself on all fours, lion-growling and staring at each other eye-to-eye in the cave made of blankets is the best way to be Jesus to our kids.

How do you most enjoy playing with your little one?

_____

_____

_____

_____

_____

_____

_____

_____

_____

_____

_____

_____

How does your child most enjoy playing with you?

_____

_____

_____

_____

_____

_____

_____

_____

_____

Play as a Foretaste of Heaven

The streets of the city shall be full of boys and girls playing in its streets.
ZECHARIAH 8:5

A Christian theologian was once asked whether it was appropriate for Christians to be playing games when there were wars and famines going on. He thought about it for a moment and then answered with a resounding "yes!" The reason he could say this with such conviction is that play is a foretaste of a heavenly reality.

The prophet Zechariah foretold a time when the streets would be full of boys and girls playing (as opposed to the current state of destruction and despair the people in Zechariah's time were experiencing). The prophet Isaiah talked about a time when infants would play near the cobra's nest (Isaiah 11:8). These strange verses remind us that in heaven we will not have fears of war, sickness, or death. There will be the beauty of forgetful play. Our children's play is an invitation to taste of this heavenly reality. It is an invitation to a momentary forgetfulness. No wonder Jesus says, "Let the children come to me; do not hinder them, for to such belongs the kingdom of God" (Mark 10:14 ESV). In their innocence they let us taste of a world that is not laden with care and pain. What an invitation to wonder we often miss when we turn down their invitations to play!

Creating with Eternal Hope

"Do not labor for the food which perishes, but for the food which endures to everlasting life, which the Son of Man will give you, because God the Father has set His seal on Him."
JOHN 6:27

The half-drunk cup of coffee is a running joke in our family. At the end of many a day, my husband will be loading the dishes into the dishwasher and will find my half-empty cup of coffee sitting cold in the microwave or resting idly on the counter. It's a sign of the many interruptions in my day as a mother: the toddler needing help at the potty, the four-year-old and the six-year-old needing conflict management again, or the baby's cry signaling time for another feed. There is a glorious inefficiency to motherhood. And sometimes it is a struggle to feel that our work has any value whatsoever when we can hardly drink a complete cup of coffee, much less finish a meaningful task.

But here's the thing: Our real work is in the eternal realm. We are caring for souls; *you* are caring for the soul of this precious toddler God has entrusted to you. As you love him, care for his physical needs, and over time guide him as he comes to understand his spiritual needs, you are working in the imperishable realm of eternity. As Jesus says, you are working for "food which endures to everlasting life," or as Paul reminded us, you are working in the realm of things that won't be burned up by the fire (1 Corinthians 3:12–15). Dishes, work deadlines, and bills—these will pass away, but your child's soul will not. You are working in the eternal realm, and your work has value beyond your wildest imagination.

Creating for an Audience of One

"His lord said to him, 'Well done, good and faithful servant; you were faithful over a few things, I will make you ruler over many things. Enter into the joy of your lord.'"
MATTHEW 25:21

Have you caught your toddler looking back at you for your smiling approval yet? Maybe they were wiggling to the music, scribbling in a coloring book, or kicking a ball, but somewhere along the way they began to learn that they love the delight of your smile. We were designed to create for the satisfaction of an audience. It is in our DNA. And whether we know it or not we are always seeking approval. There is nothing wrong with delighting others with our work and our creativity. The trouble is, too often as adults we seek out people's approval as opposed to God's approval. We work for the wrong things: the approval of others as we buy the new car, the new house, or the Disney vacation. God tells us, "Do not store up for yourselves treasures on earth, where moths and vermin destroy, and where thieves break in and steal" (Matthew 6:19 NIV). Our world values work for the feeling of importance it gives us, for ambition's sake, or for self-pride. But God tells us, "Do nothing out of selfish ambition or vain conceit. Rather, in humility value others above yourselves, not looking to your own interests but each of you to the interests of the others" (Philippians 2:3–4 NIV).

As we work, whether it's in our role as moms or in a field God has called us to or in some other creative endeavor, we must remember that we work for a different set of values, and we work to please a different audience than our peers. We work to one day hear the "well done" of our Savior. We work "heartily, as for the Lord and not for people" (Colossians 3:23 NASB 1995). We create for the applause of an audience of One, and His approval is all that truly matters.

What has your toddler created lately? Is it scribbling pictures, making sandcastles, piling blocks into a tower? What do you want to remember about the joy your little one takes in playing?

As a mother you are doing work that will last into eternity. Write a prayer asking God for His help as you do this work and that He would help you to remember how valuable your work is.

NINE
Learning

Your Twenty-Month-Old

Developmental Guide

This is the age of play and creation for your toddler as her confidence and abilities grow. Your little one is likely walking, running, and even climbing steps these days. She is probably able to hold a crayon and draw lines vertically or horizontally or scribble. She is starting to move from merely copying when playing to imaginative, pretend play. And her dexterity in stacking, doing puzzles, playing blocks, and even kicking a ball is growing. It's an incredible time to see your little one flourishing.

It's also an exhausting and messy time. Your child can burn through one activity after the next, leaving chaos in her wake. Try not to stress about the mess. Your home looks like a toddler lives there because a toddler does! Enjoy these busy days and the messy, creative person God has given you—not every season will be like this.

With that said, it will help your sanity to begin now to train your little one to play an active and happy role in tidying up. Make bins or baskets the place where things belong. And teach your little one where things go. You can make a game of cleanup by saying, "Can you find the truck? Now can you put it in the blue basket?" Or you can turn on some lively music and work together to do a fast-paced cleanup at a regular time each day.

Little ones at this age also love learning how to do things. Take advantage of this natural curiosity and their willingness to help alongside mommy by giving them little chores to do. Yes, it will take you longer now, but in the long run it will pay off. Start very simply. Let him help put the dirty clothes in a pile. Give him a wet cloth to wipe the chairs. Or allow him to help stir the pancake batter or put muffin liners into the pan. Your child will love the feeling of helping you and will be growing in his skills at the same time.

Toddler behavior can be challenging, to say the least, so when your little one is doing a nice job helping, creating, or sharing, try to praise her behavior. "I like how patiently you are waiting for Mommy to come help you," you might say. Or "Look at what a nice job you did being gentle with the doggy!" Catch her being good and celebrate it.

Developmental Focus: Cognitive Growth

As your toddler nears the second birthday, sometimes it can seem like there is an explosion of cognitive growth. Between twenty and twenty-four months, your little one will likely have mastered fifty words but will be adding new ones by the day. Here are a few other things your toddler may soon be able to do:

- Speak in short, simple sentences ("I want cup" or "Me help Mommy" or "Where going?" etc.)

- Sing songs, although words may be unclear at times
- Repeat words spoken to him or her
- Count two or three objects
- Point to different body parts when asked
- Begin to understand time and phrases like "when we go home" or "not now"
- Recognize familiar names and people in photos

You can help your toddler grow in his or her cognitive abilities by

- Counting things together: "I'm going to put three banana slices on your plate. Let's count them: one, two, three."
- Naming the colors of things: "I like your big red ball! It is so bouncy!"
- Talking about time: "Tomorrow morning we will go to the library" or "Last night you had a visit from your uncle!"
- Reading books with your toddler and naming things or interacting with the pictures: "Can you point to the mouse in the picture?" or "Let's count the bunnies on the page."

This Month's Spiritual Focus: Growing in Wisdom

Your little one is growing step by step in his cognitive development these days. Likewise, God wants us as Christians to be growing daily in our wisdom and the practical application of it. This month we'll focus on what wisdom is, where it begins, how to practically grow in wisdom, and what some of its common benefits are. We'll end the month examining a paragon of wisdom: the Proverbs 31 woman.

Holistic Growth

And Jesus grew in wisdom and stature,
and in favor with God and man.
LUKE 2:52

I treasure this verse we have about the childhood of Jesus. When it comes to the years between Jesus' birth and the beginning of His ministry, the Scriptures are relatively silent. We know His parents fled with Him to Egypt during Herod's assault on the infants (Matthew 2:16) and that they stayed there until Herod's death (v. 20), and that they returned and settled in Nazareth in the region of Galilee (vv. 22–23). And we know a story of Jesus lingering at the temple at around age twelve (Luke 2:41–51). Other than these, we really have just this one verse from Luke 2:52 that describes His childhood. But what a beautiful verse it is!

It tells us that Jesus grew in a holistic way: wisdom implies spiritual and mental growth applied to life, stature implies physical growth, favor with God implies growing close to the Father, while favor with men implies a growth in interpersonal, social connectedness. Basically, Jesus flourished. In Hebrew, the word *shalom* connotes a peaceful wholeness, a rightness and soundness of body, mind, and spirit. And this is how our Savior grew. Often I run my life through this filter. How am I doing in these areas? And as I plan a month or year ahead in my children's lives, I think through how I'm helping them grow: intellectually, physically, spiritually, and socially. What a beautiful, holistic model He gave for us and our toddlers!

The Obvious: Asking

*If any of you lacks wisdom, let him ask of
God, who gives to all liberally and without
reproach, and it will be given to him.*
JAMES 1:5

Lately, my three-year-old has been waking me up asking for "breakfasts." I think it's hilariously accurate because he eats like a hobbit throughout the morning: first breakfast, second breakfast, and sometimes he even asks me for a snack. He's a hungry little thing. My toddler, on the other hand, can't say "breakfasts" yet, but he's keeping up in the appetite department. My point is this: I get out of bed largely because of the persistent requests of this obviously hungry little boy. He asks for what he needs, knowing his mama loves him and won't ignore his pleas.

God tells us often that we should do the same. What father, when asked for bread, would give his child a stone or when asked for fish would give a snake? Jesus poses this rhetorical question and tells us, "Ask, and it will be given to you; seek, and you will find; knock, and it will be opened to you" (Matthew 7:7). And James tells us our God gives "liberally and without reproach" (James 1:5). God doesn't find fault with us for not knowing something or for needing His guidance. He doesn't roll His eyes at us and think, *Again?* He wants us to ask. He wants us to want wisdom enough to seek it like treasure, even if it costs us everything (Proverbs 4:7 NIV). So, where do you need wisdom today? Have you started with the obvious: asking?

Interceding for Wisdom

For this reason we also, since the day we heard it, do not cease to pray for you, and to ask that you may be filled with the knowledge of His will in all wisdom and spiritual understanding.
COLOSSIANS 1:9

One of the greatest things we can do for our toddlers is to intercede for them spiritually. A friend of mine recently told me about a family friend who had covenanted to pray for her sister every day of her life. What an enormous gift that friend had given to her sister! It's hard to be consistent in our prayer lives, especially for others, but Paul gives us an example here with his spiritual children of ongoing, habitual prayer.

Paul prayed that his spiritual children would grow in wisdom and understanding. He knew that this was the key to them knowing the will of God. Sometimes we think that the will of God is some great mystery when, in fact, His will is usually revealed to us in His Word. As we grow in wisdom and understanding, we also grow in the discernment of how to apply this wisdom to our lives. I suggest memorizing Colossians 1:9 and praying it daily for your toddler. Set an alarm on your phone or post the verse somewhere you will be reminded to pray. As I think ahead for my children to the time when they will be young adults, I long for them to be spiritually mature, capable of discerning God's will for their lives, and loving Him enough to apply that wisdom. Praying for our little ones daily is one of the most profound ways we can serve them.

What learning leaps has your toddler made lately?

_____

_____

_____

_____

_____

_____

_____

_____

Think again about Luke 2:52 NIV: "And Jesus grew in wisdom and stature, and in favor with God and man." Think through these categories of growth in your life. What areas do you want to ask God to help you grow in?

_____

_____

_____

_____

_____

_____

_____

_____

The Beginning of Wisdom

The fear of the LORD is the beginning
of knowledge, but fools despise
wisdom and instruction.
PROVERBS 1:7

When I was in seminary, I had the enormous privilege of studying the book of Proverbs under one of the foremost scholars on the Old Testament, Dr. Bruce Waltke. One of the translators of the NIV, Dr. Waltke wrote two exhaustive commentaries on Proverbs, and he told us that many Hebrew children would have memorized the book of Proverbs in its entirety! Can you imagine that? They took their wisdom seriously. The people of Israel saw the book as outlining a way of wisdom that they were to walk in. Proverbs is a great book for parents to read for themselves and to read to their kids as they grow. After all, these are lessons that Solomon, the wisest man on earth (aside from Jesus), wanted to pass on to his children.

Proverbs starts with this very simple yet profound lesson: Wisdom begins with the fear of the Lord. We can't truly know wisdom apart from God. Wisdom is not the same as information or intelligence. Wisdom is applied spiritual knowledge. It is practical and should be lived out. The fear of the Lord grounds this knowledge because we live our lives beneath His scrutiny, knowing we will one day stand accountable before Him. We fear God by showing reverence, awe, and respect for His absolute authority. This is something we can begin teaching our toddlers even now. We show reverence for God by teaching them not to take His name in vain. We teach them to honor God by praying with them from an early age, thanking God for every good thing He gives and asking for His help with our troubles. Even a toddler can begin to grow in wisdom as a parent models reverence and awe for our heavenly Father.

The Nature of Wisdom

But the wisdom that is from above is first pure; then peaceable, gentle, willing to yield, full of mercy and good fruits, without partiality and without hypocrisy.
JAMES 3:17

A classic toddler toy is the shape sorter. I love watching my little guy trying to unlock the mystery of the toy by putting the shape up to the hole. Try as he may, the circle won't fit the triangle spot, and the star won't budge through the square. Only the right shape fits in the right hole. In this passage, James teaches us to distinguish God's wisdom from the world's foolishness. Like the shape sorter, we are given the pattern for the shape of wisdom. As we hold the world's ways of thinking up to God's wisdom, we will clearly see where the world's thinking just doesn't align. James gives us many descriptive phrases to recognize the shape of true wisdom.

Wisdom is pure. This is the Greek word *hagnē*; it means "undivided, chaste, or pure." It is undivided in its pursuit of God's glory and can purely serve others because of it. James has just been describing the wisdom of the world, marked by bitter jealousy and selfish ambition (James 3:14). False wisdom seeks its own good at whatever cost to others. But true wisdom will not look or feel like that. It will be pure and peace-loving—promoting well-being for everyone. It will be considerate of the needs of others, submissive in the sense of being ready to take another's needs and put them before their own. True wisdom is not cutthroat favoritism, but its good fruit is found in caring for the weak. The shape of true wisdom is characterized by service for the glory of God. *Father God, help us to honestly look at our lives and see where we are trying to make the world's wisdom fit. Help us know the shape of true wisdom.*

171

The Benefits of Wisdom

Do not forsake wisdom, and she will protect you; love her, and she will watch over you.
PROVERBS 4:6 NIV

The book of Proverbs outlines a way of living that *in general* brings blessing and benefit. It is *not* a prosperity gospel. We read Proverbs within the framework of the other wisdom literature: Psalms, Ecclesiastes, and Job. Job, in particular, highlights the fact that sometimes God allows suffering to happen to the wise and righteous. But Proverbs does outline general principles of living that promote goodness and benefit to the listener. They keep the listener from folly and often death.

Here are just some of the benefits of wisdom's ways you will find in the book of Proverbs: A wise person will live in safety (1:33), store up victory (2:7), taste pleasure and peace (3:17), enjoy intimacy with God (3:32), experience clear paths (4:12), see success (8:14), receive respect and honor (11:16), flourish (11:28), and have security for her family (14:26). The benefits go on. I don't have space to list them all. Again, these are not guarantees of health, wealth, and prosperity but are general principles that show wisdom brings these kinds of benefits. What's our takeaway? We can be confident as we teach our toddlers God's ways. Walking in the way of wisdom is walking in the way of life and peace. It is the very best way of life we can offer them. Yes, God sometimes allows deep hardship to interrupt the natural benefit flow of wisdom, but it is always for His specific, good purposes in our lives. As we teach our children to walk in wise ways, we can have assurance that good will come from it.

When does your little one experience frustration most often?
How do you help your toddler through it?

_____

_____

_____

_____

_____

_____

_____

_____

_____

Can you think of any benefits your toddler may be experiencing
because you are seeking to walk in the way of wisdom?

_____

_____

_____

_____

_____

_____

_____

_____

Finding Wisdom in His Word

Prize her highly, and she will exalt you;
she will honor you if you embrace her.
PROVERBS 4:8 ESV

We could all take a lesson from toddlers in how to be active. If they aren't constantly walking, running, or climbing, we wonder if they are sick! In fact, studies out of Duke and Northwestern universities found that toddlers expend 50 percent more energy than adults (adjusted for body size) and that 40 percent of that energy is consumed by their brains.[4] God wants us to be active like our toddlers, especially with our minds.

In the opening chapters of Proverbs, we see all the strong action words used to communicate how diligently we should search for wisdom. Solomon told us that we should treasure it, call out for it, raise our voice for it, seek it like silver, and search for it like hidden treasure (2:1–4). In Proverbs 4, wisdom is to be loved, treasured, pursued, prized, guarded, embraced, and not forsaken.

You can see that God does not want us to be neutral about wisdom; He wants us to actively pursue and love wisdom. One of the ways we do this is through diligent study of the Word. As Paul reminded Timothy, "All Scripture is breathed out by God and profitable for teaching, for reproof, for correction, and for training in righteousness" (2 Timothy 3:16–17 ESV). We can go to our study of the Word with confidence that the Spirit will give us exactly what we need to grow in wisdom through it. Sometimes the Spirit will use the Word to rebuke us, sometimes to encourage us, and sometimes to train us. But always, if we seek wisdom diligently in God's Word, we can expect God to help us grow!

Finding Wisdom
Among the Wise

Listen to counsel and receive instruction,
that you may be wise in your latter days.
PROVERBS 19:20

Outside of your family, who do you turn to for advice most often? What are they like? Would you characterize them as wise, peace-loving, considerate, merciful, and sincere? These are some of the characteristics of wisdom given to us by James that we looked at earlier in this study (3:17). If these aren't words you'd use to describe the people you rely on the most, perhaps it would be good to pray that God would provide you some deep companions like this.

The book of Proverbs is very concerned with the kind of company we keep. The wise walk with the wise; they are not companions of fools or, worse, the wicked. "He who walks with wise men will be wise, but the companion of fools will be destroyed" (13:20). When we walk with the wise, we are strengthened: "As iron sharpens iron, so one person sharpens another" (27:17 NIV). When we walk with hotheads, we run into the danger of growing like them (22:24–25). Now, this doesn't mean that we should shun the company of those outside the faith. Jesus was a friend of sinners, prostitutes, and tax collectors. And likewise, God wants us to befriend all kinds of people, being His light to them. But moms, when it comes to who we turn to for counsel, support, and soul-company, He wants us to choose wisely that we may grow wise. Not only will this have a profound soul-shaping effect upon us but it will also affect our toddlers, as they grow up seeing models worthy of emulating. Surround yourself and them with people of wisdom that you may grow wise together.

Finding Wisdom Among the Aged

Is not wisdom found among the aged?
Does not long life bring understanding?
JOB 12:12 NIV

I'm so blessed to have two prayer partners who are older than me. These beautiful women of God have finished raising their children. They've walked through the years I'm currently in and have survived them! They've made it through sleepless nights, teething, temper tantrums, potty training, terrible twos, thousands of questions from their preschoolers, grade-school years, teenage mood swings, and college applications. They've held the hands of their parents as they faced aging and some as they've faced death. They have battle scars and laugh lines from the journey. I love being with them because they have a way of putting my crisis du jour into perspective: this too shall pass.

In Titus 2:4–5, Paul urged older women to train the younger women in how to love their husbands and children. It's not that older people are the only ones to whom God has given wisdom. Sometimes young people can be quite astonishing in the wisdom God has given them. And it's not that every person who is gray with age is necessarily wise, but sometimes with life experience come perspective and decades of seeing the faithfulness of God. Do you have some older godly women in your life that you talk to on a regular basis? If not, I encourage you to begin praying that God would show you some with whom you could seek out a deeper relationship. Also remember that you are an older woman to someone you know. Ask God if there is someone younger He wants you to befriend.

Does your toddler have any buddies? Who are his or her friends? What are they like?

_____

_____

_____

_____

_____

_____

_____

We've talked a lot this week about the company we keep. Who is someone wise in your life that you really appreciate? What is this person like? Why would you encourage your child one day to find a friend or mentor like this?

_____

_____

_____

_____

_____

_____

_____

The Wise Woman Blesses Her Husband

The heart of her husband safely trusts her;
so he will have no lack of gain. She does him
good and not evil all the days of her life.
PROVERBS 31:11–12

I know some women have an adversarial relationship with the Proverbs 31 woman. Personally, class lectures and commentaries from one of the foremost biblical scholars on the book of Proverbs, Dr. Bruce Waltke, have made me come to love her. In his commentary on the book, Dr. Waltke points out that the Hebrew word *chayil* in verse 10, often translated as noble, is closer to valiant.[5] The form of the poem itself follows a pattern called a *panegyric*—a kind of poem written in praise of a battle hero, an ode to a warrior. This woman is strong; but she is strong *for the sake of others*, which is perhaps the most beautiful kind of strength there is. It is a strength poured out. As mothers to toddlers, constantly giving, we see a worthy model here and a validation that our work is valiant work.

Proverbs 31 was also written as a chiastic poem, a symmetrical poem that forms a kind of X. Chiasms helped communicate a writer's main point—putting that heart of the poem in the center. The center of this poem reads, "Her husband is known in the gates, when he sits among the elders of the land" (v. 23). And the point here is that this valiant woman is so capable (managing the household, her cottage industry, the vineyards) that she frees her husband up to influence the community for good. It's not that this woman loses her identity. She uses her strength to bless her household, the poor, her husband—and through her husband the world at large. Her reach is legendary.

178

The Wise Woman Blesses Others

She extends her hand to the poor, yes, she reaches out her hands to the needy. She is not afraid of snow for her household, for all her household is clothed with scarlet.
PROVERBS 31:20–21

Was the Proverbs 31 woman a real person? Scholars disagree. Some say she is the personification of wisdom. Others say she might be the great-great-grandmother of Solomon—Ruth, the wife of Boaz. Whether she is real or a model, she is held up as the ideal of the life of wisdom. True wisdom overflows in blessing for others. And we see this in the cascade of blessing that flows from this joyful woman. I say joyful because the work of her hands in verse 13 could be most literally translated as making her palms glad.[6] She laughs at the days ahead (v. 25) because she knows that by wisdom she has provided for her family, her servants, and the poor who come to them.

She clearly works hard, getting up early (v. 15), staying up late (v. 18), purchasing fields, planting them (v. 16), and selecting wool and flax (v. 13) and making it into clothes and bedcoverings (vv. 21–22). But her work brings her joy because through this practical wisdom she blesses everyone around her. Whether or not the Proverbs 31 woman was a specific, real woman or an amalgam of many, we can learn from her that there is joy in doing something we love for the sake of others, joy in serving, and joy in wisdom. From her we can catch a vision as mothers that there is important work to be done for the kingdom, both inside and outside of our homes, and that there is joy as we commit our lives to being a source of God-centered blessing to others!

The Wise Woman Is Blessed

Her children rise up and call her blessed;
her husband also, and he praises her.
PROVERBS 31:28

I have said it before, but it merits repeating that Proverbs does not teach a prosperity gospel—that is, the idea that God's people are always blessed with wealth, health, and success. There are plenty of verses in Proverbs that indicate sometimes the wise know want: "Better is a little with the fear of the LORD, than great treasure with trouble" (15:16), or "Better a little with righteousness than much gain with injustice" (16:8 NIV). These Scriptures, along with others, and the whole of the wisdom literature (Job's suffering, for example, or the persecutions experienced by the psalmist) remind us that though wisdom often brings blessing, it is not always in the form of financial, physical, or social gain.

With that said, we do see that wisdom often brings tangible blessing. In the Proverbs we find the hard worker often has food, while the lazy goes hungry. And in chapter 31, we see some of the blessings the wise woman herself enjoys as a benefit of her wisdom. Her husband and children are happy in her—they literally stand in her presence and praise her (vv. 28–29). She enjoys "the fruit of her hands" and "her own works praise her in the gates" (v. 31).

Caring for the needs of a toddler is often a thankless job. While our little ones can't thank us now, Proverbs 31 gives us hope that perhaps one day they will.

Is your toddler climbing, running, jumping, dancing, or balancing on one foot these days? What new skills are you seeing?

_____

_____

_____

_____

_____

_____

Serving others can be draining, yet it can also bring us joy. What do you think makes the difference in whether service feels life-giving or life-stealing? If serving is not giving you joy right now, pray for God to help change that.

_____

_____

_____

_____

_____

_____

_____

_____

TEN

Sharing

Your Twenty-One-Month-Old, Developmental Guide

Your toddler is a bundle of energy these days! Most twenty-one-month-olds can run, squat, throw a ball underhand, and climb. Sometimes she has so much energy, she literally doesn't know what to do with it. Help your little one burn off that energy with some active adult-led play. If you can get outside for a game of chase or tag, go for a walk, or play at the park, it will help. And it's also great to get your little one into the habit of being physically active (and outdoors!) from an early age. That will continue reaping benefits well into her older years.

You may also notice your toddler has some strong preferences these days. That's all part of his growing autonomy and it's nothing to be afraid of. When it's wise, respect your child's preferences. But when it comes to things like nutrition, offer healthy choices rather than give in to demands for sweets or junk food. Giving choices empowers your little one within boundaries. So let him choose whether to wear the red or blue shirt or to play blocks or dinosaurs or go to the library or park. But also help him realize that some things, like issues of safety, are nonnegotiable.

Language is likely blossoming this month as your child is putting together more and more two-word phrases. Continue to help by narrating activities and reading plenty of books to help add to that growing vocabulary. It's also a great time to make sure that vocabulary includes great words like "Please!" "Thank you!" and "Sorry!" Also, the more you can give your toddler vocabulary for emotions, the easier managing those feelings will be.

Your child may also be managing teething pain this month with lower second molars erupting, causing some discomfort. Sometimes this pain can be mistaken for an ear infection because of the location of the pain. If your child needs something soothing, this is a great time for a cold smoothie, soft mashed bananas, smooth soups or stews, or even frozen fruit like grapes or cherries (just make sure they are cut into small pieces, and remove any pits or seeds).

Developmental Focus: Taking Turns

While sharing and turn-taking may seem like the same thing, sharing is actually a much more complex collaborative process that is more developmentally appropriate for a preschooler. At around age two, however, most toddlers can begin to get the concept of turn-taking with lots of support from parents. Turn-taking teaches your child to listen to the needs and feelings of another and respond with empathy. If your child has other siblings at home (or will have them soon), you may need to work on these skills earlier. There are some things you can do to help support them in this goal.

Rather than using a timer or strong-arming the sharing arbitrarily, help guide your kids with simple requests and responses. Your toddler may not be ready for long sentences yet, but you can teach him to say something like "Turn, please!" Longer sentences can increase feelings of frustration and may be out of their range at this point, so it's okay to keep it simple.

The other child may say, "Sure," or if engrossed in play may say, "When I'm done." You may need to support the waiting child during the interval, by introducing another toy or activity to help pass the time. You can reinforce with children that turn-taking isn't the same thing as keeping a toy forever. It means one child will play and then the next and so on.

How can you support turn-taking early in your home? Incorporate it in lots of everyday ways so that it's not a new concept when it comes up with a friend or sibling. For instance, when putting together a puzzle, you can say, "Let's take turns putting in pieces. First you, then me." When making something, you can say, "Let's take turns putting in ingredients. You dump the sugar. Then I'll crack the eggs." Or when playing outside, "Let's take turns rolling the ball. First, I'll roll it to you. Then you roll it to me."

This Month's Spiritual Focus: Sharing

Like our toddlers, we need encouragement in learning to share and be generous. God loves a generous heart. This month we'll focus on how generosity, hospitality, and compassionate serving not only please God but further the gospel's reach.

Sharing: Foundational Views

I have no need of a bull from your stall or of goats from your pens, for every animal of the forest is mine, and the cattle on a thousand hills. . . . If I were hungry I would not tell you, for the world is mine, and all that is in it.
PSALM 50:9–10, 12 NIV

Toddlers and big kids alike are going to squabble over toys. Mine did and yours will too. Sometimes when my children are arguing over who should have a toy, I gently remind them, "Well, you know the toy doesn't actually belong to either of you."

Before we begin this devotional series about sharing our resources as adults, it's helpful to pause and consider to whom our resources really belong. Everything you and I have—every dollar in our bank accounts, our homes, our cars, our possessions, our talents, our intellect, even our children—are gifts given to us by God. In essence, they are on loan. He owns it all! In this passage in Psalm 50, God reminds us that He doesn't *need* anything from us; it is *His* already.

When we are caught up in worldly possessiveness, this fact should throw us off balance in a good way. It should remind us that if it's all His anyway, then He should have first and last say about how we prioritize using our resources. It also begs the question, if He doesn't *need* our gifts, why does He call us to be generous and lend freely? Ponder that question today, and we'll consider it more closely in the days to come.

Why Give?

But whoever has this world's goods, and sees his brother in need, and shuts up his heart from him, how does the love of God abide in him?

1 JOHN 3:17

Yesterday I left you with a question: If God owns everything and can make another entire universe on a whim, why does He ask us to give? Did you think about it?

The answer to this question is not primarily practical but theological. God asks us to give because this is the nature of love. God is love. And love gives. As we grow in likeness to love, we will want to give because love is giving. Love overflows. God gives us the opportunity to give because He wants us to experience more of His nature. He wants us to know Him not just intellectually but experientially, by being like Him.

So giving is really an invitation to an experiential knowledge of God. Mind-blowing, isn't it? In one sense, all the opportunities your toddler affords you to give without getting anything in return are invitations to know God, not just with a head knowledge but with the knowledge of hand and heart. Likewise, as we extend that compassion and mercy to people beyond our household, we are getting more than we give. We are getting the chance to know God in that deep way of experiencing Him through likeness. Giving is a sign of the reality of God's love rooted in our hearts.

Giving Changes Us

"Do not lay up for yourselves treasures on earth, where moth and rust destroy and where thieves break in and steal; but lay up for yourselves treasures in heaven, where neither moth nor rust destroys and where thieves do not break in and steal. For where your treasure is, there your heart will be also."
MATTHEW 6:19–21

You may be beginning to teach your toddler about sharing or taking turns. Likely, one of your motivations in this is not just for peace in your house or on the playground but because deep down you know what kind of person you want your son or daughter to be. You want your toddler to grow to be a person of empathy and kindness, right?

God could certainly supply our neighbor's needs, but He is also concerned about our hearts. He wants to use the opportunities to give in our lives to *change us*! Here in the Sermon on the Mount, Jesus tells us that where our treasure is, our heart is also. Treasure and heart go together. What we treasure reveals our heart! Just like when your child offers that toy to a friend, it shows your child values the friend more than the toy. God wants to see the allegiance of our hearts shift. And how we think about possessions is one of the best barometers of our allegiance that there is. When we are focused on building our own mini-kingdoms here and now, our focus is not on the eternal things God says matter most. Giving is God's opportunity to us to change our minds, hearts, and priorities.

Who are some of your toddler's playmates these days?

_____

_____

_____

_____

_____

_____

_____

_____

_____

Love gives. Who is someone who has often given to you? How do you see the love of Christ in this person?

_____

_____

_____

_____

_____

_____

_____

_____

Giving Is a Heart Check

Command those who are rich in this present world not to be arrogant nor to put their hope in wealth, which is so uncertain, but to put their hope in God, who richly provides us with everything for our enjoyment.
1 TIMOTHY 6:17 NIV

Yesterday we meditated on how giving changes our hearts. Paul also picked up this theme in his letter to Timothy, explaining that giving is a heart-check for us. It shows us where we are putting our hope. This is especially true for those who "are rich in this present world," who often forget who is behind all the bounty we enjoy. Most who live in the first world fall into this category: we aren't scouring the earth for insects to eat for protein or crying out in hunger asking God for a meal. Often our needs could more rightly be termed "wants."

For those "rich in this present world," God wants us to give as a way of remembering our hope is not in our possessions, and it's not in whatever is on our latest want list—the beautifully decorated playroom for our toddler, the new outfit, the week at the beach, or the private preschool education. Our hope is in God. And He is the very One "who richly provides us with everything for our enjoyment." And finally, God wants us to "do good, to be rich in good deeds, and to be generous and willing to share" in order to "lay up treasure . . . for the coming age, so that [we] may take hold of the life that is truly life" (vv. 18–19 NIV). Giving changes us because it helps us put our value on the eternal. It helps us lay hold of the life that is truly life, not the counterfeit gods of comfort and worldly approval that compete for our hearts.

Giving Out of Gratitude

Now it came to pass when the king was dwelling in his house, and the LORD had given him rest from all his enemies all around, that the king said to Nathan the prophet, "See now, I dwell in a house of cedar, but the ark of God dwells inside tent curtains."

2 SAMUEL 7:1–2

Since they were just tiny tots, my boys have never passed a flower without the impulse to pick it and give it to Mommy as a gift. Every dandelion, daisy, or even the weed that looks more flowery than weedy is a candidate. I love it and always accept these offerings as the treasures they are: gifts from the heart. What a beautiful model for me to imitate—a heart longing to give.

As Christians, we should find the generosity of God and His gracious abundance in our lives overwhelming. I love this translation of Ephesians 1:3: "Every spiritual blessing in the heavenly realm has already been lavished upon us as a love gift from our wonderful heavenly Father, the Father of our Lord Jesus—all because he sees us wrapped into Christ. This is why we celebrate him with all our hearts!" (TPT). No wonder we want to celebrate Him. Generosity begets gratitude, and gratitude begets generosity.

David was overwhelmed with a desire to build a temple for God because of the abundance and kindness God had shown him. Mary broke an alabaster jar for Jesus out of overwhelming gratitude for His mercy toward her. Sometimes we give because we are just so overcome with gratitude we must show it.

191

Giving to Jesus

"For I was hungry and you gave me food, I was thirsty and you gave me drink, I was a stranger and you welcomed me, I was naked and you clothed me, I was sick and you visited me, I was in prison and you came to me."
MATTHEW 25:35–36 ESV

Your toddler is getting to the age where he is developmentally able to engage in pretend play. In many ways, his imagination is coming alive. When it comes to giving, God also asks us to use our spiritual imagination. Here, Jesus tells us that when we share (whether it's food, drink, clothing, hospitality, physical care, or companionship), we are to use our spiritual imagination to see our giving as unto Him.

This certainly empowers us to see our service in a new light. Not only are we serving the person in need, but also we are serving Christ. If we feel overwhelmed with gratitude for all that Jesus has done for us on the cross, we have a chance to give directly to Him. We are invited to look on the poor, the sick, the lonely, and the imprisoned and see the face of Jesus. Solomon wrote something similar in Proverbs: "Whoever is generous to the poor lends to the LORD, and he will repay him for his deed" (19:17 ESV). When we remember that God needs nothing from us, we can understand this in its proper light. Somehow, in God's economy when we give to the least, the last, and the lost, we are giving to the One who made and loves them and knows their needs.

Have you noticed your little one being kind or generous? What have you praised her for lately?

_____

_____

_____

_____

_____

_____

_____

In what ways are you "rich in this world"? Perhaps it's with your finances, with a home, with an abundance of talents, time, creativity, or connections? How is God calling you to give of your abundance?

_____

_____

_____

_____

_____

_____

_____

_____

Giving to Be Seen?

*"Take heed that you do not do your
charitable deeds before men, to be
seen by them. Otherwise you have no
reward from your Father in heaven."*
MATTHEW 6:1

Has your toddler ever tried to melt you with a smile or a kiss after doing something naughty? If he hasn't yet, it's coming. You see, no one really has to teach us how to manipulate. We somehow just figure out that we can use good things, even service, for our own ends.

The Bible is clear that there are plenty of wrong reasons to give. We can give for the empty praise of men. We can give to feel pride in how generous we are. We can give to make someone feel indebted to us or to get ahead. There are countless ways we can be self-serving even in our service.

But God tells us again and again that He doesn't look at outward appearances but at our hearts. He wants us to give not for praise or recognition from man but out of love for Him. He wants us to give to an audience of One, Himself. It begs the question: Where are we getting our sense of self-esteem or self-worth? If the answer is anyone or anything but God, we need to repent and ask for God to help us serve for the only reason that matters: our love for Him.

Giving in Secret

"But when you do a charitable deed, do not let your left hand know what your right hand is doing, that your charitable deed may be in secret; and your Father who sees in secret will Himself reward you openly."
MATTHEW 6:3–4

In honor of St. Nicholas Day (December 6), my kids and I started a fun little family tradition. We call it "drive-by gifting." Basically, we sneak up on our friends' homes and leave them a gift and a note about the real St. Nicholas and his love for giving in secret. We ring the doorbell and then run and hide before they can see us. I have to say that it has been the very best addition to our Christmas holiday season we've made. The kids *love* every bit of it, though later on they are just dying to tell their friends it was us. There is something in our human nature that craves recognition for our service.

I think that's why God gives us this warning. He knows that it would be easy to serve people for the wrong reason. Giving in secret is a way to check our hearts. It's a way to make sure we are giving for the right reason. It's not that God doesn't want us to enjoy praise. We are told He will one day say, "Well done, good and faithful servant" (Matthew 25:21). He just wants to be the One to give us our "Atta girl!" He wants our hearts to be right, and the best way to do that is to keep our lips tight.

Giving Cheerfully

So let each one give as he purposes in his heart, not grudgingly or of necessity; for God loves a cheerful giver.
2 CORINTHIANS 9:7

I asked my three-year-old to return the toy car he had taken from his older brother. After tears, he angrily threw the car at his brother's feet. That's when I said, "Let's try that again." That's because attitude matters just as much as action. If a child needs time and a guided conversation with Mommy to get his heart in the right place before we try again, we do it. But we usually try to rewind and do it the right way before moving on.

God doesn't want our begrudging, complaining giving either. He doesn't want us rolling our eyes and writing a check. He wants us to give cheerfully.

So what do we do if we aren't there? We may need to just stop and pray. Perhaps we need to ask God to show us what is clogging our compassion. Maybe we are too busy, and we need God to help us figure out what in our lives needs to go. It could be that we are afraid we don't actually have enough, and we need to pray for a heart of faith. Or maybe we are resentful that someone else is getting served when we feel like we could really use a little help. God doesn't want us to give begrudgingly. He wants to *change* us through giving. And if we aren't giving cheerfully, let's stop and see why.

How do you and your toddler bond? What are things you do together that you truly enjoy?

_____

_____

_____

_____

_____

_____

_____

_____

This week we've focused on how we give and whether or not we are doing it for the right motivation. Write about a time when you gave for the right reasons. How did that feel?

_____

_____

_____

_____

_____

_____

_____

_____

Giving in Faith

*There is a lad here who has five
barley loaves and two small fish, but
what are they among so many?*
JOHN 6:9

I love it when my children lead me in unexpected ways to Jesus. Sometimes when we sit around the dinner table at night and my husband asks one of our children to pray, it is all I can do to hold back tears. One will say a prayer for a friend suffering cancer, or a buddy whose parents are divorcing, or for "all the bad guys in the whole world to become good guys." I love how their simple childlike faith leads me to Jesus afresh.

In this story of Jesus feeding the five thousand, I am so often moved by this child's simple act of faith. People are hungry and he has more than enough. He sees simply that he can share, and he wants to. He approaches the good Teacher's followers.

Who knows what the boy expected. But we do know that the boy didn't let the magnitude of the problem paralyze him from answering the Master's call. He just responded in faith and left the rest to Jesus. How marvelously surprising to see how Jesus takes this generous yet humble resource and multiplies it. He transforms the gift offered in faith. Isn't it beautiful?

Where are you letting the magnitude of the problem paralyze you from acting in faith? It's not a big problem to Jesus. What do you have that He's calling you to offer in faith?

Entertaining Angels Unaware

Do not neglect to show hospitality to strangers, for thereby some have entertained angels unawares.
HEBREWS 13:2 ESV

My mom has often shared a story of my granddad picking up a hitchhiker and bringing him home. The hitchhiker, who was trying to get a lift across country to see his son, was very advanced in years, and he was so weak and frail that he could barely climb into my granddad's pickup. Before my granddad bought the man a bus ticket, he brought him home, gave him the dignity of a place to bathe and sleep, clean clothes (while my grandmother took his soiled ones and washed and hung them out to dry), and he even trimmed the man's wild hair and scraggly beard.

I never knew my granddad, but I cherish this story of his generosity of heart expressed through hospitality. And when I think of entertaining angels unaware, I often wonder about that frail old man.

Hospitality played a key role in the spread of early Christianity. Today, I think hospitality is a dying art. Often hosts care more about impressing people than blessing people. And yet consider how many people you know who are starved for real loving care. God invites us to be people of hospitality perhaps because He knows that we need our hearts opened wider than the needs of just ourselves and our family. And hospitality is something that most of us—even moms with toddlers—can do. You don't have to have a model home or a gourmet meal to be hospitable. In fact, someone you know may need to be invited into your mess to see that your life isn't perfect, to feel the freedom to be vulnerable with you.

199

The Refreshment of Giving

*A generous person will prosper; whoever
refreshes others will be refreshed.*
PROVERBS 11:25 NIV

I have six children, and sometimes—I'll be honest—when we get a good snow, I'd rather cuddle up inside with hot cocoa and a good book than go to all the trouble to find then yank on six pairs of snow pants, six fluffy jackets, six pairs of gloves, six pairs of boots, and six hats. Oh, and don't forget the lip balm! Oh, and did you go potty? After all that work, the idea of getting myself likewise bundled and then crunching my way with them to a good sledding spot seems like way too much effort. But here's the thing: nearly every time I do it, I come home aching from laughter, refreshed by the joy in their spirits, the newly fallen snow, and the fact that I've just made a memory with them that will last a lifetime.

In God's economy, often when we refresh others, we find ourselves refreshed. We see this principle over and over again when it comes to giving. He who "sows generously will also reap generously" (2 Corinthians 9:6 NIV). Or "Good will come to those who are generous and lend freely" (Psalm 112:5 NIV). Or as Jesus says, "Give, and it will be given to you. . . . For with the measure you use it will be measured back to you" (Luke 6:38 ESV). We don't give to get. But when we give, God often has a way of giving us back more than we gave.

Getting my six kids ready to go out in the snow is hard work, but worth the effort. What has been hard work lately with your toddler, but well worth the effort involved?

_____

_____

_____

_____

_____

_____

_____

_____

_____

Write about a time where your giving or service refreshed your own spirit.

_____

_____

_____

_____

_____

_____

_____

_____

_____

ELEVEN
Obeying

Your Twenty-Two-Month-Old,

Developmental Guide

Your twenty-two-month-old is growing in independence and learning many new skills this month, but he still longs to know you're nearby and paying attention. That's why interruptions are the name of the game. Try not to be annoyed by them, and instead realize they are little moments when your toddler wants to connect. Use these interruptions as opportunities both to bond and to teach polite words like "please."

Speaking of new skills . . . your toddler may be able to kick a ball, walk backward, and maybe even balance on one foot while holding onto something sturdy. Standing on tiptoes is another skill your little one may master around this age. You may need to take a look around the house to see what those extra few inches mean in his ability to reach objects that have been previously out of reach on a counter or shelf.

Speaking of reaching new heights, your toddler may be able to follow more simple instructions these days as her receptive language (words she understands) continues to grow. Directions can move from one to two or possibly three steps as understanding and memory grow.

Consequently, you may notice your little one is listening and repeating you more these days. She mimics not only your words but also your tone. So it's a good time to think about not just what words come out of your mouth but also how you are saying them.

All that listening and repeating means that it's also a great time to introduce simple nursery rhymes or songs that can help expand your child's vocabulary and boost memory skills. There are great resources available today to also introduce Scripture memory through song at an early age. What a great time to help your little one expand vocabulary, strengthen memory, and learn about the love of God.

Finally, your twenty-two-month-old might be showing signs of potty-training readiness. You can start encouraging him to sit on the potty. But don't put too much pressure on your toddler too soon. Many kids aren't ready to learn until they are closer to twenty-seven to thirty-two months.

Developmental Focus: Managing Behavior

Let's face it: training a toddler is tough business. But somewhere between the ages of eighteen and twenty-four months your child needs to begin to recognize, understand, and respect parental authority. This should happen, however, within a context of love, grace, and connection. A lot of parenting with toddlers is not so much discipline as it is managing behavior. Let's think through some things you can be doing.

First, a little forward-thinking on your part can help prevent misbehavior before it happens. Make sure you have enough time built into your day, especially for transitions between activities. Ensure your little one is well-fed and rested, taking time to connect relationally each day, especially one-on-one. This can go a long way toward preventing many of the problems before they even arise.

Next, offering options is a way to empower your toddler in his growing autonomy while also cutting down on the inevitable power struggles. Giving your child choices within the boundaries of your authority gives him feelings of independence and safety. Think ahead about points where power struggles may be occurring and think through what options you can offer. For instance, "It's time for bed. Do you want to walk up the stairs ahead of me or have me fly you up like an airplane?" You are communicating the boundary (bedtime) while offering an empowering choice.

Don't underestimate the power of supervision. Your little one still needs lots of guidance and support. Your presence is a powerful tool. That doesn't mean solving all his problems. It does mean being tuned in and attentive to the frustrations and sources.

Finally, your toddler needs to know what your expectations are and what the consequences (when appropriate) are if she doesn't follow them. Keep your expectations clear and simple. Establish eye contact when you are communicating and use simple words and motions to make sure she understands.

This Month's Spiritual Focus: Obedience

Just as your little one is learning what it means to obey and walk under your authority, you also are growing in your ability to listen well to God's Word, apply it, and walk in His ways. This month we'll focus on obedience, God's discipline in our lives, and the reason for it.

Obeying God: Parent Under Authority

God placed all things under his feet and appointed him to be head over everything for the church.
EPHESIANS 1:22 NIV

This month as we think on the topics of obedience and discipline in our lives as we relate to God, we will see so many implications for how we parent our toddlers and growing children. A great place to start is with the fact that even as adults, you and I are people under authority. We answer to God. God has put everything under Jesus' authority—that includes us! And it includes how we parent. One day we will answer for our own obedience in this life generally, and also as parents particularly.

While the Bible clearly gives parents authority over their children (Ephesians 6:1), it also definitively sets parents in the context of being under God's own authority (Psalm 47:7–8). We are charged with teaching our children to obey all that God has commanded (Deuteronomy 11:18–19; Psalm 78:5). We are specifically told not to embitter them (Ephesians 6:4; Colossians 3:21). We are instructed to provide for them (2 Corinthians 12:14). We are instructed to set a good example for them (Genesis 18:19). We are to reflect God's love and compassion (Isaiah 66:13; Psalm 103:13; Luke 11:11). And we are to discipline them in love (Proverbs 29:17).

As people under authority, we can model what it means to honor God and the other authorities He's put in our lives. To honor means to show respect and regard. It speaks to not just our actions but our attitudes. Growing our toddlers in loving obedience begins with our own hearts being submitted to God's authority.

Obeying a Perfect Father

*I will be a Father to you, and you shall be My
sons and daughters, says the* LORD *Almighty.*
2 CORINTHIANS 6:18

None of us had perfect parents, nor will we be perfect parents. But if
you are God's child today, you have a perfect Father. He gives us a model
to strive after as we parent. Looking at the character of our Father God
tells us a lot about what kind of character we should have toward our
children. Let's consider briefly our Father's heart.

We have a loving Father. In fact, the whole earth is full of His unfailing love (Psalm 119:64). We have a Father who protects us (John 17:11–12),
provides for us (Matthew 6:8), comforts us (Isaiah 51:12), forgives us
(Micah 7:18–19), counsels us (1 Kings 22:5), teaches us (Psalm 32:8–10),
disciplines us in love (Hebrews 12:5–11), tells the truth (Isaiah 45:18–19),
encourages us (Psalm 10:17–18), will never abandon or betray us (37:25),
and listens to us before we even call (Isaiah 65:24). He is compassionate
and patient (Psalm 145:8), faithful (57:10), always fair (9:8–10), and trust-
worthy (145:13). In short, He is perfect.

And His amazing perfection should fill us with motivation to obey,
knowing His heart toward us is goodness itself. It should also inform the
kind of parent we want and aim to be. While none of us will be perfect,
we can still strive to be godly in our parenting style, knowing that even
when we fail we can point our kids to the fact that they, too, have a God
who is a perfect Father.

Obedience and Our Good

*But he said, "Blessed rather are those who
hear the word of God and keep it!"*
LUKE 11:28 ESV

E arlier in this book, we spent some time looking at the perfections of God's laws—laws that are sweeter to our senses than honey—and the goodness of God's commands for us. With the psalmist we can declare, "The boundary lines have fallen for me in pleasant places; surely I have a delightful inheritance" (Psalm 16:6 NIV). Or we can take Jesus at His word, that those who hear God's Word and keep it are blessed.

When we consider obedience, we need to understand that the things God is calling us to obey offer us life, goodness, and wholeness. Likewise, as we call our children to obey, we shouldn't present some list of arbitrary whims that bring us more peace and quiet, whims that are all about Mommy's comfort, indulgence, or clean home. Like our heavenly Father, we must call our children to obey God's laws, which are sweet to our spirits and good for our souls. And it is our job to help them understand that we are asking them to obey the good things that we ourselves obey because they are good for us and because our heavenly Father loves us and wants our best. We are obeying together.

What is something you've been teaching your toddler lately?

_____

_____

_____

_____

_____

_____

_____

_____

What does it mean to you to know that you have a perfect
heavenly Father?

_____

_____

_____

_____

_____

_____

_____

Motivation for
Obedience: Loving God

*"I do as the Father has commanded me, so that
the world may know that I love the Father."*
JOHN 14:31 ESV

My toddler has recently learned how to blow kisses. He puts his little hand to his lips, makes a "mwah" sound, and then blows a kiss in my direction. Meanwhile, my preschooler has begun blurting out at the most random times (and highest volumes), "Mommy, I love you so much in the whole world!" These little acts of love just melt my heart. It seems all the love we've poured into our little guys sometimes just spontaneously overflows.

Obedience is hard for all of us—toddlers and parents alike—but in one of the most foundational senses we obey because we love. In this poignant scene in the upper room, Jesus set the example. Within the next few hours, His ordeal would begin. Judas would betray Him with a kiss, armed soldiers would surround Him by torchlight, and His adversaries would haul Him before the authorities to begin mocking, insulting, scourging, and ultimately crucifying Him. Jesus would meet His adversary: "I will no longer talk much with you, for the ruler of this world is coming" (John 14:30 ESV). There was about to be a showdown. Who would rule Jesus' heart? Jesus had no doubt in His heart what would happen: Satan had no claim on Him (v. 30). He would obey the Father, showing the whole world His love for Him (v. 31).

Notice that to Jesus, obedience boils down to loving the Father and showing the world that love. He obeys the Father because He knows He loves Him, and He can trust the Father's heart.

Motivation for Obedience: God's Renown

"Let your light so shine before men, that they may see your good works and glorify your Father in heaven."

MATTHEW 5:16

For good or bad, sometimes our children's obedience or lack thereof reflects on us. This is why we cringe in the checkout line when our toddler is throwing a fit over a candy bar, and why we also beam when our child is the one who shares with a friend who is sad. As parents, we have to resist the urge to discipline out of shame or embarrassment, remembering our ego is not saddled to the whims of a toddler, but our worth is hidden in Christ.

But as Christians, we can be motivated to obey God as an active way to bring glory to the Father. Jesus tells us that as we let our light shine—as we obey God's commands and walk in His ways of love, mercy, and kindness—people will glorify the Father. Peter put it in terms of being careful, not giving evildoers an opportunity to accuse us of wrong but a reason to "glorify God" (1 Peter 2:12). And Isaiah was already drawing this connection centuries before when he said, "Yes, Lord, walking in the way of your laws, we wait for you; your name and renown are the desire of our hearts" (Isaiah 26:8 NIV). Obeying God is a way of bringing Him renown.

If we love God, we want to see His reputation go forth. We want others to notice God's goodness and glorify Him. We want to see other worshippers brought into the joy.

Motivation for Obedience: A Future Reward

But without faith it is impossible to please Him, for he who comes to God must believe that He is, and that He is a rewarder of those who diligently seek Him.
HEBREWS 11:6

L et's be honest. All of us are motivated at some level by rewards. Perhaps your toddler is motivated by star stickers on the potty chart. Or maybe your older children do chores in part because they know it puts a jingle in their pockets. And you and I might go for an early jog for our health or to button our prepregnancy pants. We are motivated by rewards, intrinsic and extrinsic, and that's a part of life.

God doesn't want us to obey *only* for rewards, but He isn't ignorant of how rewards motivate us. Paul said, "If in this life only we have hope in Christ, we are of all men the most pitiable" (1 Corinthians 15:19). His point is that we have hope in eternal life and a future beyond battered bodies. In other places God talks openly about rewards for those who seek him (Hebrews 11:6), how those who have sacrificed in this life have a hope of greater bounty in the world to come (Mark 10:29–30), and how the Lord will reward us for whatever good we've done (Ephesians 6:8).

So while God wants us to obey out of love, He also wants to motivate us with a future hope. This is part of the reality of obedience. Obedience begets blessing: sometimes in this life, but always in the life to come.

What mischief or mayhem has your toddler caused that you can laugh about?

_____

_____

_____

_____

_____

_____

_____

_____

Jesus obeyed God in the very hardest thing—going to the cross—out of love for the Father. How does God's love motivate you in the hard things?

_____

_____

_____

_____

_____

_____

_____

_____

Child Training and Fatherly Love

Have you completely forgotten this word of encouragement that addresses you as a father addresses his son? It says, "My son, do not make light of the Lord's discipline, and do not lose heart when he rebukes you, because the Lord disciplines the one he loves, and he chastens everyone he accepts as his son."
HEBREWS 12:5–6 NIV

I train my toddler because I love him. Because I love him, I teach him not to put his fingers in the wall socket. Because I love him, I teach him to look both ways before we cross the street. Because I love him, I teach him to treat others with kindness, gentleness, and respect. And because I love him, I will correct him and allow certain consequences when he does wrong. But because I love him, all of this will be bound up in love, covered in love, motivated by love, tempered by love.

Discipline is a word that causes some of us to bristle. Perhaps it's been used wrongly in our lives. But it is a word the Bible uses here in Hebrews to communicate encouragement to us. God disciplines, or trains, us because He loves us, because we are His sons and daughters. A father doesn't pay this kind of special attention to other people's sons and daughters; he trains his own children to be good and wise and strong because they are his. The writer of Hebrews wants us to take heart—to be encouraged—that when God disciplines us through circumstances, it's because He cares enough to make us more like Him.

God Corrects with Words and Actions

My son, do not despise the LORD's discipline, and do not resent his rebuke, because the LORD disciplines those he loves, as a father the son he delights in.
PROVERBS 3:11–12 NIV

Y ou are stepping into the parking lot with your toddler by the hand, and suddenly he squirms out of your grip and starts to run. Chances are you are going to do two kinds of training in the next few minutes. First, if you can reach him, you'll grab him by the hand and pull him out of danger. You will take action. Second, you'll explain to him with your words why he needs to stay close by. You may take further steps, but you will at least do these two things to train your child.

God also disciplines us with words and actions. In this Proverb, two different Hebrew words are used: *yasar* (discipline), which includes God's actions; and *yakach* (rebuke), which denotes God's words. Similarly, in Hebrews 12:5, which we looked at yesterday, we are encouraged not to make light of God's actions and not to lose heart at His words of rebuke. In our lives, God may correct us with words (*yakach*) of conviction from His Word, from the pulpit, from a friend or spouse, or through the Holy Spirit. Meanwhile, His actions of rebuke (*yasar*) may take a number of forms. Whether it's redirecting our paths away from evil, allowing us to feel the consequences of our sinful actions, or permitting suffering or hardship to enter our lives, He is always using these things for redemptive purposes. Whether it's words or actions, they come to us because of His Fatherly love and attention to shaping our character.

The Fruit of Discipline

*Now no chastening seems to be joyful for the
present, but painful; nevertheless, afterward
it yields the peaceable fruit of righteousness
to those who have been trained by it.*
HEBREWS 12:11

Have you ever spent time with someone's older children who are simply a joy to be around? I love being with my nieces and nephews because they are so polite, helpful, fun, and in tune with the needs of others. But I know that they didn't get this way by some dumb luck or their parents going with the flow. Their parents have poured into them through training, instruction, correction, modeling, and perseverance, and now I get to benefit from the fruit of lots of years of spiritual growth.

The writer of Hebrews knew that in the short term, discipline just isn't pleasant. For parents, it's easier in the short term to do nothing with our toddlers, to go with the flow, to just not handle the issues. But in the long run, harvests do not happen without work. Harvests require preparing the soil, planting seeds, frequent watering, weeding, and attention to the needs of the growing plant. They require the farmer to stay close, to exercise attention and effort. The farmer must have a vision for the harvest or he or she would never endure the work. Likewise, in our lives we submit to God's discipline because we know He can see how to get to the harvest. And when it comes to parenting, if we want to taste the fruit one day of kids who are a joy to be around, we've got to endure the hard work of training.

Developmentally, your toddler is learning to follow more complex directions. It's a fun time to introduce simple games like Simon Says, for example, which can also help with listening skills necessary in obedience. What games have you taught your child or would like to teach him soon?

_____

_____

_____

_____

_____

_____

In our last devotion, we thought about how a vision of the harvest helps us with the hard work of discipline and training. What's your harvest vision? What kinds of character traits are you hoping to see formed in your child?

_____

_____

_____

_____

_____

_____

_____

Our Struggle to Obey and Theirs

For what I am doing, I do not understand. For what I will to do, that I do not practice; but what I hate, that I do.
ROMANS 7:15

I love how honest Paul (who seems like a super-saint to us) is here in this Bible verse. Haven't we all thought, *I don't understand what I'm doing. The things I want to do—will to do—I don't practice. The things I hate, I do.* Goodness, I've been there. I struggle a lot with accepting criticism. I know how I want to respond to criticism: with grace and kindness, knowing that when my husband or someone who loves me brings something up, it's because they want to help me. Yet so often when it happens, I get defensive. I hear my tone of voice. I sense my body language, and it's not what I want—not what I will. I have to work hard to lower my defenses and remember that the person speaking to me is trying to help me and to accept that criticism with grace and humility.

Here's the point: First, let's be honest with God at the points where we struggle. Let's not hide but ask honestly for His help to change us from the inside out. But second, as appropriate, let's be open with our kids as they grow. "You know what, sweetie? I see how hard you are trying to obey and how it's not going well. I want you to know Mommy struggles too. I struggle to be kind when someone is mean to me. This is why we need Jesus so much!" Use every opportunity you have like this to talk about our need for grace. And emphasize *our.* You and your child need the grace of God to walk in obedience. We are all sinners in need of grace.

The Sorrow, Repentance, Forgiveness Rhythm

Now I rejoice, not that you were made sorry,
but that your sorrow led to repentance. For
you were made sorry in a godly manner, that
you might suffer loss from us in nothing.
For godly sorrow produces repentance.
2 CORINTHIANS 7:9–10

As we strive to obey Christ fully, we really shouldn't be surprised by the sin in our lives and hearts. We have an enemy inside (the flesh) and two enemies outside (the world and the devil). As we grow as Christians, we shouldn't be surprised by our sin, but hopefully we are truly sorrowful about it, letting that sorrow lead us to repentance and that repentance to His forgiveness and grace. Again and again, the Scriptures remind us that we are debtors who need forgiveness. God's Word also reminds us that we are debtors who often see other people's debts and miss our own. We are people who can spot the speck in our brother's eye and miss the plank in our own (Matthew 18:21–35 and 7:5). All this is really important as it relates to parenting.

As we discipline our own children, we can do it either as demanding hypocrites or as humble fellow sinners in need of grace. Hopefully, as we coach our own children, it will be as people who know this rhythm of sorrow, repentance, and forgiveness well. It will be as people who are so familiar with our own need for forgiveness that we can have true compassion for another's need. I pray that we won't be parents who exult in being speck-finders in our children's eyes while plank-ignorers in our own.

Training Together

*So I do not run aimlessly; I do not box as one
beating the air. But I discipline my body and
keep it under control, lest after preaching
to others I myself should be disqualified.*
1 CORINTHIANS 9:26–27 ESV

We have friends from church who hold records in the running world. Currently, the mom holds the record for fastest indoor relay in the women's over-forty category, while the son holds the record for the fastest high school mile. The mom has coached the son as well as many others for years. And while she has years more experience as both a coach and a runner, both she and her son have a mindset of training and improving.

I think this is the attitude we need to adopt as we raise our children. Yes, right now you are raising a toddler—and training a toddler isn't like training a teenager—but as your child grows, you should see yourself as both a coach and a more experienced runner, but a runner nonetheless, a runner in the same race. That means you are a coach who can empathize with the hard work of training, with the pain, discomfort, and sacrifice involved, and with the temptations to quit. Parenting from a point of grace and empathy, as one further along in the journey, opens the door to understanding and communication in a way that parenting from a perspective of feigned mastery never can.

Is your toddler stringing more words together these days? Does your little one mispronounce certain words in a cute or memorable way? What do you hope to remember about your child's communication these days?

_____

_____

_____

_____

_____

_____

How do you think your own ongoing need for grace and forgiveness, repentance and obedience, discipline and perseverance will shape how you parent?

_____

_____

_____

_____

_____

_____

_____

TWELVE
Dressing

Your Twenty-Three-Month-Old, Developmental Guide

It's hard to believe that just a year ago you carried that chunky little baby of yours wherever he wanted to go. Now your toddler has probably become leaner, having grown a few inches and lost those cute baby rolls. (The average twenty-three-month-old girl weighs 25.9 pounds and is 33.7 inches tall; while the average boy is 26.3 pounds and 34.2 inches tall.) And while you were lugging that baby around at eleven months, now at twenty-three months he is likely walking, running, and jumping.

Not only that, but his verbal abilities have grown by leaps and bounds. He likely has a vocabulary of more than fifty words and may have closer to one hundred. He strings two to four words together to make simple sentences. What a wondrous year of growth it has been!

And that sleepy little baby, who gave you two solid naps, is likely a thing of the past; your toddler is probably down to one nap a day lasting about one and a half hours or less and sleeps at night for about twelve hours.

She may be driving you crazy asking you to sing or replay a song over and over again or to read that favorite picture book every night.

Toddlers love repetition, so embrace the phase, keeping in mind that your little one is learning and processing through this repetition and is savoring the predictability of it. While you may be ready for bigger and more varied things, she may still love simplicity.

Speaking of simple, with your toddler's second birthday just around the corner, you may be thinking about the best ways to celebrate. While she will likely love the balloons, candles, cake, and presents, keep in mind that big parties can be overwhelming for kids this age. Lots of noise and people generally are. Small, simple, and short is probably the best recipe for toddlers. But if you do decide to go all out, make sure your little one is well rested and keep your expectations low for the guest of honor. You have a lifetime ahead for larger and more involved parties if that is something you enjoy planning.

Developmental Focus: Dressing and Self-Care

Your toddler's burgeoning independence is showing itself in a lot of ways these days. She may show an interest in learning to do things for herself. This is a good age to start teaching those self-care skills.

She may want to dress herself but will likely still need a lot of help until about two and a half. While she may have mastered undressing, dressing actually involves quite a few cognitive skills, fine motor skills, and gross motor skills, so working on it together is a great way to help her increase dexterity and empower her with newfound abilities.

In terms of cognitive skills, you can help your little one think through seasons and what kinds of clothes we wear in different seasons.

You could use magazines to cut and paste different kinds of clothes onto pages decorated with pictures of winter, spring, summer, and fall. Or if you have dolls and clothes around the house, practice laying out clothes for them for the right season.

Your toddler also needs to understand the order of operations. While this comes easily and without thought for us, for her there is some learning involved to think through the necessary steps to get clothes in the right order. As you help her dress, narrate the actions with signal words like *first*, *second*, *third*, and *fourth*.

In terms of gross motor skills in dressing herself, your child is learning to lift one leg while balancing on another. You can help her master this earlier by teaching her to sit down while pulling on bottoms. Show her how to determine front from back.

She can also work on developing mastery of the many fine motor skills involved with dressing. You may be able to find some toys or busy books that encourage hands-on practice with zippers, buttons, and snaps.

As your child masters all of these skills, it will be a tremendous boost to her confidence. Remember as she works on these skills that they are complex for a toddler, and celebrate her little accomplishments and her effort even when she appears with a shirt on backward or a sweater in the middle of summer.

As we continue thinking about how we as children of God grow in grace, the Bible returns often to the metaphor of clothing and of clothing ourselves in Christ. This month we'll focus on what we learn about God through this metaphor and how to clothe ourselves in Him.

The First DIY Flop

Then the eyes of both of them were opened, and they knew that they were naked; and they sewed fig leaves together and made themselves coverings.
GENESIS 3:7

It's snowing and mid-January when out prances my preschooler, proudly dressed in his green swim shirt and blue Hawaiian swim trunks. He thinks he's ready for the day. I know he's completely underdressed. (While your toddler probably isn't quite to this point yet, he may be undressing with a little too much ease for your peace of mind, especially if diapers are still necessary!)

Like my preschooler, post-fall Adam and Eve bumbled out into the open in their self-made outfits. Like my preschooler, they were completely unprepared for the elements. They came face-to-face with their nakedness for the very first time. They were guilty, ashamed, vulnerable, defenseless, and humiliated, and the worst part is that they thought they could handle it themselves. Their DIY efforts, however, were a total flop. How could these fig leaves stand up to the wear and tear of traveling outside the hospitable realm of the garden and into a world where they would toil among the thorns and thistles and break ground and bring harvest by the sweat of their brows? The leaves couldn't stand up. They wouldn't. They would fall apart. We see in this our first introduction to the recurring image of clothing in the Bible. We see that their spiritual nakedness was going to need a covering that Adam and Eve could not provide themselves. They needed a more substantial solution. They needed someone to help and something that would last.

Dressing His Children

Also for Adam and his wife the LORD God
made tunics of skin, and clothed them.

GENESIS 3:21

Adam and Eve soon discovered that their DIY solution wouldn't cut it. They needed a covering that would cost something beyond precious: a life. This animal skin is our first record of a sacrifice for sin in the Bible. An innocent animal had to pay the penalty of Adam and Eve's transgression. And we see in this a foreshadowing of Christ Himself, who would one day be our perfect atoning sacrifice.

But for now, we see here the incredible care of God. He Himself— after this great betrayal—would dress His children. He would provide the sacrifice. And He would piece together a gift, a reminder of His ongoing love, presence, and provision, which would be so close to them that it would be like a second skin. He would do this *for* them—dress them because He loved them. He hadn't abandoned them.

I have in the past year or so really come to love the symbolism of clothing in the Bible. I love that God covered Adam and Eve with a reminder of His sacrifice that was so close to them, they would have felt it surrounding them all day long. I love that this symbol of His love for them covered them, that it came between them and the thorns and thistles of this fallen world. I love that there was not a moment of the day when they didn't feel this tangible touch of His protection, provision, and promise on their skin and get reminded to stop and marvel.

Miracle Clothes

"I have led you forty years in the wilderness.
Your clothes have not worn out on you, and
your sandals have not worn out on your feet."
DEUTERONOMY 29:5

Sometimes as moms of toddlers, it feels like our kids are constantly outgrowing clothes. By the time we figure out how to snap the pajamas with two dozen snaps in all kinds of strange places, they've outgrown them. By the time the season is just right for those adorable little overalls, she's too tall to fit into them. And leave it to a toddler to figure out a way to destroy in less than an hour with this morning's blueberry pancakes that darling outfit your old Sunday school teacher hand-embroidered. What we need for them are some of those wilderness miracle clothes— clothes that don't wear out no matter what.

Haven't heard of the wilderness miracle clothes? Well, they kind of get overshadowed by the plagues, the parting of the Red Sea, the manna, the quail, the water from the rock, and all those splashier Exodus miracles. But there it is—a quiet little miracle we moms can appreciate—nestled in the midst of all those bigger ones. For forty years of wandering, their clothes and shoes did not wear out. What's the point here? First, the clothing points to God's provision for them. Second, it points ahead to a covering that God plans to give us that won't perish or fade—a covering in Christ that we will wear for eternity and that will never fade, soil, or tear. We, too, are dressed by our Father in miracle clothes—a covering that will never be too torn or worn to wear.

Do you have a favorite little outfit you like to dress your toddler in or perhaps a favorite he or she has outgrown? Do you have any clothes for your child that are extra special because they've been handed down a generation or have some other special significance?

_____

_____

_____

_____

_____

_____

God wants to be as close to us as a second skin—that's the idea we glean from His use of the symbol of clothing in the Old Testament and the New Testament. How does it make you feel to realize God wants this kind of closeness with us?

_____

_____

_____

_____

_____

_____

_____

Filthy Garments

*But we are all like an unclean thing, and
all our righteousnesses are like filthy rags;
we all fade as a leaf, and our iniquities,
like the wind, have taken us away.*
ISAIAH 64:6

It's not too often that a child comes in so filthy that I pick him up and haul him directly to the tub. But sometimes it does happen, like when we visit this particular farm the kids love in the muddy season. I don't even let them pass go. We go directly to the tub when we get home, and Mommy carries them! And yet this is good, clean fun compared to our passage from Isaiah.

This passage is about clothes that are ceremonially unclean. These might be clothes like those that belong to a leper—someone whose flesh was literally rotting off their body—or the bloodstained rags of a woman in menstruation. God says our righteous deeds—our very best deeds—are like filthy rags of this sort.

We once had a skunk crawl under our front steps and die. The stench infected our house for weeks. We hired a professional to dig out the carcass and haul it away. Then my husband poured bleach into that hole to further try to cleanse the stench. And yet the odor of that skunk held on to my husband for days afterward. This is the point: To God, even our most noble acts without Him reek. There is no way we could ever come into the presence of a holy God like this. We need to be washed and changed.

Fairy-Tale Transformations

*I will greatly rejoice in the LORD, my soul
shall be joyful in my God; for He has clothed
me with the garments of salvation, He has
covered me with the robe of righteousness, as
a bridegroom decks himself with ornaments,
and as a bride adorns herself with her jewels.*

ISAIAH 61:10

Toddlers are a great excuse for busting out our favorite childhood fairy tales such as Goldilocks, Red Riding Hood, Thumbelina, and, of course, Cinderella, the classic story of total transformation.

But while Cinderella goes from soot-covered sister in the cinders to the exquisite creature who appears in a ball gown and glass slippers, our transformation in Christ is even more stunning. We go from the stench of our unclean rags to the wonder of Christ's robes of perfect righteousness. And here in this prophetic passage in the book of Isaiah, the prophet foretold a day when God's people will wear "the garments of salvation" and "the robe of righteousness." The stench of our uncleanness is washed away and we are not just dressed in a set of clean clothes but arrayed in the finest clothes possible, like the set we wore on our wedding day. This is a fairy-tale transformation if there ever was one. Only in our case, it is no fairy tale at all but reality itself, the true story of the gospel. Praise God today for your new garments—garments of salvation—a ball gown better than Cinderella's finest! Are you still seeing yourself as an ash-stained maid or do you now think of yourself as a cleansed daughter of the King? It matters.

From Sackcloth to Gladness

*You have turned for me my mourning into
dancing; You have put off my sackcloth
and clothed me with gladness.*
PSALM 30:11

My boys can change out of fancy clothes faster than a hot knife can slide through butter. They tell me that they are scratchy and uncomfortable. Clothing is the one thing that touches our body constantly. If it's uncomfortable, it's hard to think of anything else.

In the time of the Israelites, people sometimes wore such uncomfortable clothing on purpose. Sackcloth was usually made out of very coarse black goat hair or camel hair. It was worn around the waist like a loincloth so it would have touched one's most intimate parts, making it an outward, constant, uncomfortable reminder of an inward state. Traditionally, sackcloth was worn for mourning, in submission to a hostile entity (1 Kings 20:31–32), or out of grief and self-humiliation (2 Kings 19:1).

While we don't wear sackcloth and ashes today, it is a reminder that we should truly, deeply mourn our sin and that some griefs cannot be hidden. And here it demonstrates that God does not want us to stay in such grief forever. He wants to change us out of these clothes. He wants to give us garments of praise—to clothe us with gladness. Why? So that we might sing His praise and not be silent. Has God forgiven you? Then He has changed your sackcloth to garments of gladness! Has He restored you from sin or deep grief? Give Him thanks today for how He changes our clothes.

Are you starting to think about your toddler's second birthday? What plans do you have or hope to make to celebrate this great milestone?

_____

_____

_____

_____

_____

_____

_____

How has God changed your clothes for you? Has He changed you from filthy rags to robes of salvation or from sackcloth to garments of gladness? Testify to His goodness in not leaving you but changing you!

_____

_____

_____

_____

_____

_____

_____

Clothed in Christ

All of you who were baptized into Christ
have clothed yourselves with Christ.
GALATIANS 3:27 NIV

If you are like most moms of toddlers, undoubtedly you have a favorite comfy outfit that you love to put on, especially when you don't have to go anywhere. If there are comfort foods, certainly there are comfort clothes. Maybe it's those super-soft pajamas, the yoga pants, or the jeans and sweatshirt you'll never, ever throw out. Cashmere or cotton, fleece or flannel, we all have our favorites.

In some ways the metaphor of being clothed in Christ is perhaps one of the strangest. Here in Galatians, it says if we have been baptized into Christ, then we have clothed ourselves in Christ. In other words, if we have followed Christ in repentance and belief and in this outward sign of an inward reality, then Christ covers us, surrounds us, envelops us. The image of being clothed in Christ is truly an intimate one and one I think God wants us to cherish. He should be as close as second skin to us, constantly engaging our senses. There are so many levels on which this metaphor works. Think about how a sports team is identified by their uniforms; you can't mistake them on the field. Likewise, we are to be unmistakably His. Consider how comfortable you are in your favorite clothes. Likewise, Jesus is our comfort, our peace. Remind yourself how some clothes protect us and how Jesus comes between us and the enemy. And think of how certain clothes transform you. Jesus is better than any reality makeover. Be mindful today, every time you look at your clothes, that Jesus is closer; He surrounds us.

Inside or Outside?

To them God willed to make known what are the riches of the glory of this mystery among the Gentiles: which is Christ in you, the hope of glory.
COLOSSIANS 1:27

In yesterday's devotion we looked at Galatians 3:27, which says, "for all of you who were baptized into Christ have clothed yourselves with Christ" (NIV). The waters of baptism surround us on every side like clothing, covering us with Christ. We meditated on this image of being clothed in Christ and all the beautiful implications of this metaphor. But there are numerous other places in Scripture where it talks about Christ *within* us, like Colossians 1:27, which says, "Christ in you, the hope of glory," and Galatians 2:20, which says, "It is no longer I who live, but Christ lives in me." So which is it? Is Christ *within* me or *around* me? Are the gospel writers just unable to make up their minds?

I love that this is one of those cases not of either-or but of both-and. Perhaps this prayer attributed to St. Patrick in the fifth century puts it best: "Christ with me, Christ before me, Christ behind me, Christ in me, Christ beneath me, Christ above me, Christ on my right, Christ on my left." Isn't it amazing to think of Christ surrounding us and within us? We are not just next to Christ, but He is within us. We have true union with Him, just as He has true union with the Father: "I in them, and You in Me; that they may be made perfect in one" (John 17:23).

Putting Off the Old

*Put off, concerning your former conduct,
the old man which grows corrupt
according to the deceitful lusts.*
EPHESIANS 4:22

I've seen friends who have shed lots of weight and who rid their closets of clothes that are several sizes too big. It looks absolutely liberating—to say goodbye to a former way of living and embrace a new, healthier version of oneself. The closest I've come to that is giving away my maternity clothes (ironically, only to have to borrow some back a few years later).

In several places in the New Testament epistles, we are told to put on Christ, to put on humility (1 Peter 5:5), to put on love (Colossians 3:14)—to wear them like garments. But just as we must teach our toddlers, there is an order of operations in getting dressed. We can't put on the new until we take off the old. And this is exactly what Paul instructed in Ephesians 4:17–32. These clothes no longer fit the new man. It's time to cast them off! Paul was specific. Here are the things that are worn out and need to be moved out of the closet: "deceitful lusts" (v. 22), lying (v. 25), stealing (v. 28), corrupt talk (v. 29), and "bitterness, wrath, anger, clamor, and evil speaking be put away from you, with all malice" (v. 31). Friend, these garments don't fit you anymore. It's time to take them off and put them on the trash heap. In Jesus, you get a whole new wardrobe. And trust me; it looks a whole lot better on you than these rags!

As you look back on the past year and how your toddler has grown, what stands out to you the most? What changes have brought the most joy? What special moments do you want to remember?

_____

_____

_____

_____

_____

_____

_____

_____

We've spent some time this week meditating on the image of being clothed in Christ. We've talked about comfy clothes, uniforms, protective clothes, and transformational clothes. Which of these aspects of being clothed in Christ speaks to you most?

_____

_____

_____

_____

_____

_____

Clothed in Humility

All of you, clothe yourselves with humility toward one another, because, "God opposes the proud but shows favor to the humble."
1 PETER 5:5 NIV

Have you ever specifically pictured Jesus around babies and toddlers—perhaps holding a baby in His arms or playing peekaboo with a little boy or girl about the age of your child? In one of His most moving lessons, Jesus scolded His disciples for trying to keep such little ones away when the parents were seeking His blessing upon them. Instead, Jesus drew one such child to the forefront and said, "Truly I tell you, anyone who will not receive the kingdom of God like a little child will never enter it" (Luke 18:17 NIV). Clearly, Christ thinks that we have something to learn from our littlest ones—something incredibly profound.

Children are dependent by nature. They are not in control of their lives. They need protection and provision. Whether they realize it or not, whether they act like it or not, children are humble. It is in this poverty that they teach us, likewise, to clothe ourselves "with humility," as Peter described it. The greatest in the kingdom is the one who has no pretense of power but who realizes his dependence on God in all things. God has most graciously given us little ones who can daily remind us how to receive the kingdom of heaven. Just as our children look to us, we look to God in dependence. We clothe ourselves in humility when, like little children, we cry out and live expectantly, trusting God for our needs to be met. As we learn greatness from our children's humility, we can, in turn, be humble in our interactions, realizing our dependence and frailty helps us realize our brother's also.

Clothed with Strength

She is clothed with strength and dignity;
she can laugh at the days to come.
PROVERBS 31:25 NIV

I s your little one already outgrowing those overalls and footed pajamas you bought just a few months ago? Are the little shoes you spent a pretty penny on quickly getting too tight? There is something about how quickly our kids grow that can make us nervous about finances and the future. Will we be able to keep up with the needs of tomorrow?

As we come to the close of this devotional, I want to return again to the Proverbs 31 woman, an example for us as mamas in how to live with a peaceful heart in the midst of constant and ever-changing needs. Notice that in verse 21, which we looked at earlier, "She is not afraid of snow for her household, for all her household is clothed with scarlet." How is it that she can look ahead to the season of hardship and not be afraid? The answer is twofold. She has not been idle, and her trust is in the Lord. We see how hardworking this mama is in verses 16 through 19; we see how this woman makes the most of her time, her intellect, and her skills. It can be said of her, "She watches over the ways of her household, and does not eat the bread of idleness" (v. 27 ESV).

But ultimately, she can laugh at the days to come because her hope is in the Lord. She is to be praised because she is "a woman who fears the LORD" (v. 30). Strength of heart comes from such wise and righteous living and deep trust in God. Dignity comes from knowing God has made us in His very image, and we are truly valuable because of this. Sweet mama friend, clothe yourself in this kind of strength and dignity for the days ahead; it is your inheritance as a daughter of the King of kings.

Putting On Immortality

For we who are in this tent groan, being burdened, not because we want to be unclothed, but further clothed, that mortality may be swallowed up by life.
2 CORINTHIANS 5:4

Mamas, as we come to the close of this book and of this focus on being clothed in Christ, I want to call you to persevere courageously because we have an unshakable hope. Our lives will not be easy if we follow hard after Jesus. We will face frustration, suffering, and persecution. What gives us hope to wake up day after day, and love and teach and train our little ones to love Jesus? What gives us hope to keep trusting Jesus in the face of suffering? And when one day our bodies—like everyone else's—begin to break down, what gives us hope to keep being a joyful light to the next generation, telling of His mercies to our children and grandchildren?

Here Paul told us that we groan inwardly, knowing that we long to be clothed in immortality. We are not meant for time but for eternity. The reason we wish our happy moments with our toddlers, or spouse, would last forever is because we are meant for forever. So when you feel the wistfulness of wishing you could make time stand still, remember we have that longing because we were made for eternity. And when those moments of pure sweetness with your toddler happen, enjoy them as foretastes of a coming unstoppable and imperishable joy. The wonder of it is that the joy we try so hard to hold in our hands—true joy—won't be passing away; one day it will be ongoing. We will take off this mortal body and put on immortality; death will be swallowed by life (1 Corinthians 15:54). Until then, keep holding fast to the One who holds fast to you.

I feel like I've been on a journey with you! It hardly seems possible that your toddler is about to turn two! Take a moment to celebrate how you've seen your little one grow and blossom this year. What joys and special moments of this toddler year do you hope to always remember?

_____

_____

_____

_____

_____

God has equipped you with everything you need for living a godly life (2 Peter 1:3). That means He has already given you everything you need to be a godly mom. Write a note here to yourself to walk in the confidence and hope of one who is called and equipped—clothed and ready, through the grace of Christ, for whatever comes her way.

_____

_____

_____

_____

_____

Notes

1. John Piper, "God Is Always Doing 10,000 Things in Your Life," *Desiring God*, January 1, 2013, https://www.desiringgod.org/articles/god-is-always-doing-10000-things-in-your-life.

2. Chana Stiefel, "What Your Children Learn by Imitating You," *Parents*, October 5, 2005, https://www.parents.com/toddlers-preschoolers/development/behavioral/what-your-child-learns-by-imitating-you/. Note that this URL now links to another article.

3. Diane Benoit, "Infant-Parent Attachment: Definition, Types, Antecedents, Measurement and Outcome," *Paediatrics & Child Health* 9, no. 8 (October 2004): 541–45, https://www.ncbi.nlm.nih.gov/pmc/articles/PMC2724160/.

4. Ann Gibbons, "Little Kids Burn So Much Energy, They're Like a Different Species, Study Finds," *Science*, August 12, 2021, https://www.science.org/content/article/little-kids-burn-so-much-energy-they-re-different-species-study-finds.

5. Bruce Waltke, *The Book of Proverbs: Chapters 15–31*, The New International Commentary on the Old Testament (Grand Rapids: W. B. Eerdmans, 2005).

6. Waltke, *The Book of Proverbs*.

About the Author

After graduating with a master's degree in biblical studies, Catherine Claire Larson spent seven years writing with Chuck Colson for BreakPoint radio, *Christianity Today*, and *Newsweek* online. Today, she writes amidst the clatter and curiosity of six young children.